Listening to Life

Psychology and Spirituality in the Writings of Frederick Buechner

To Judith —
Thank you for joining our class.
Keep listening!
Victoria S. Allen

Victoria S. Allen

American Literary Press, Inc.
Five Star Special Edition
Baltimore, Maryland

July 31, 2007   Chautauqua, NY

Listening to Life: Psychology and Spirituality in the Writings of Frederick Buechner

Copyright © 2002 Victoria S. Allen

All rights reserved under International and Pan-American copyright conventions. No part of this book may be reproduced, stored in a retrieval system, or transmitted in any form, electronic, mechanical, or other means, now known or hereafter invented, without written permission of the publisher. Address all inquiries to the publisher.

Library of Congress
Cataloging-in-Publication Data
ISBN 1-56167-726-4

Library of Congress Card Catalog Number:
2001119485

Cover photo courtesy of Buechner Collection, Bushwell Memorial Library, Wheaton College (IL)

Published by

American Literary Press, Inc.
Five Star Special Edition
8019 Belair Road, Suite 10
Baltimore, Maryland 21236

For

David,

who taught me about listening to life

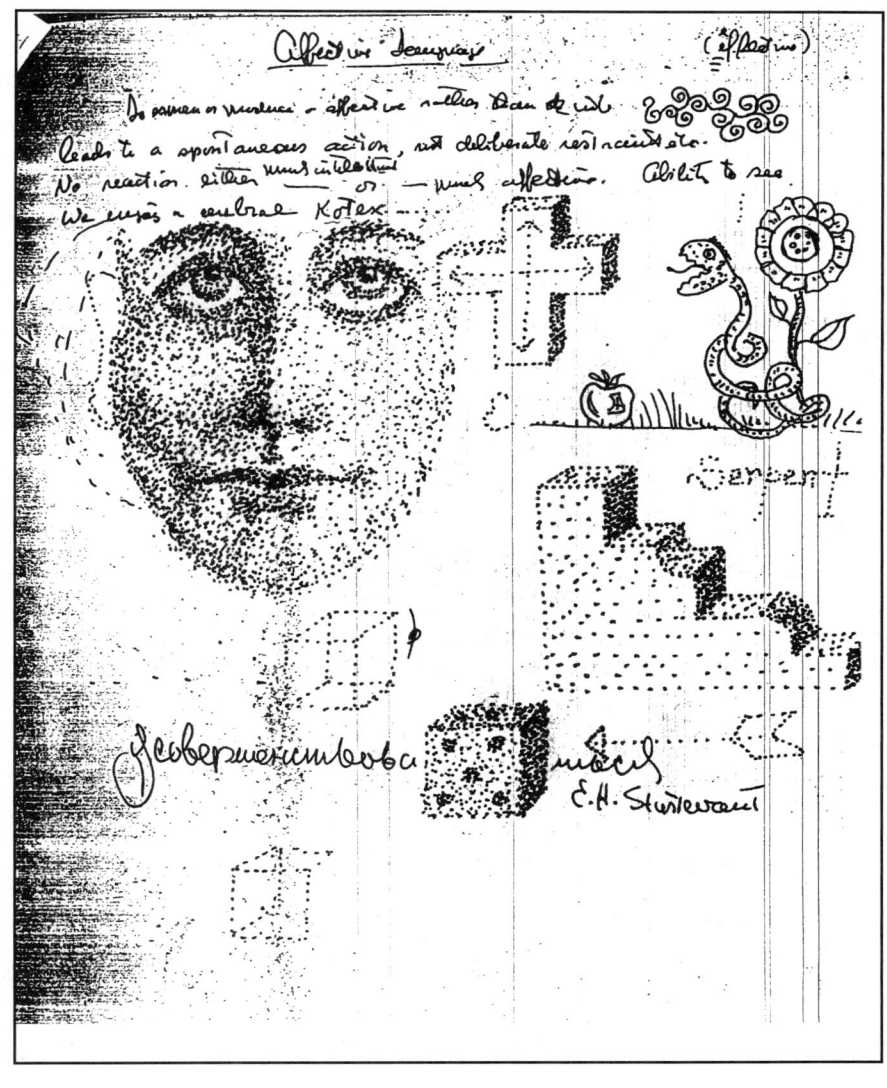

Doodles from Frederick Buechner's Princeton Notebooks
Buechner Collection, Buswell Memorial Library, Wheaton College (IL)

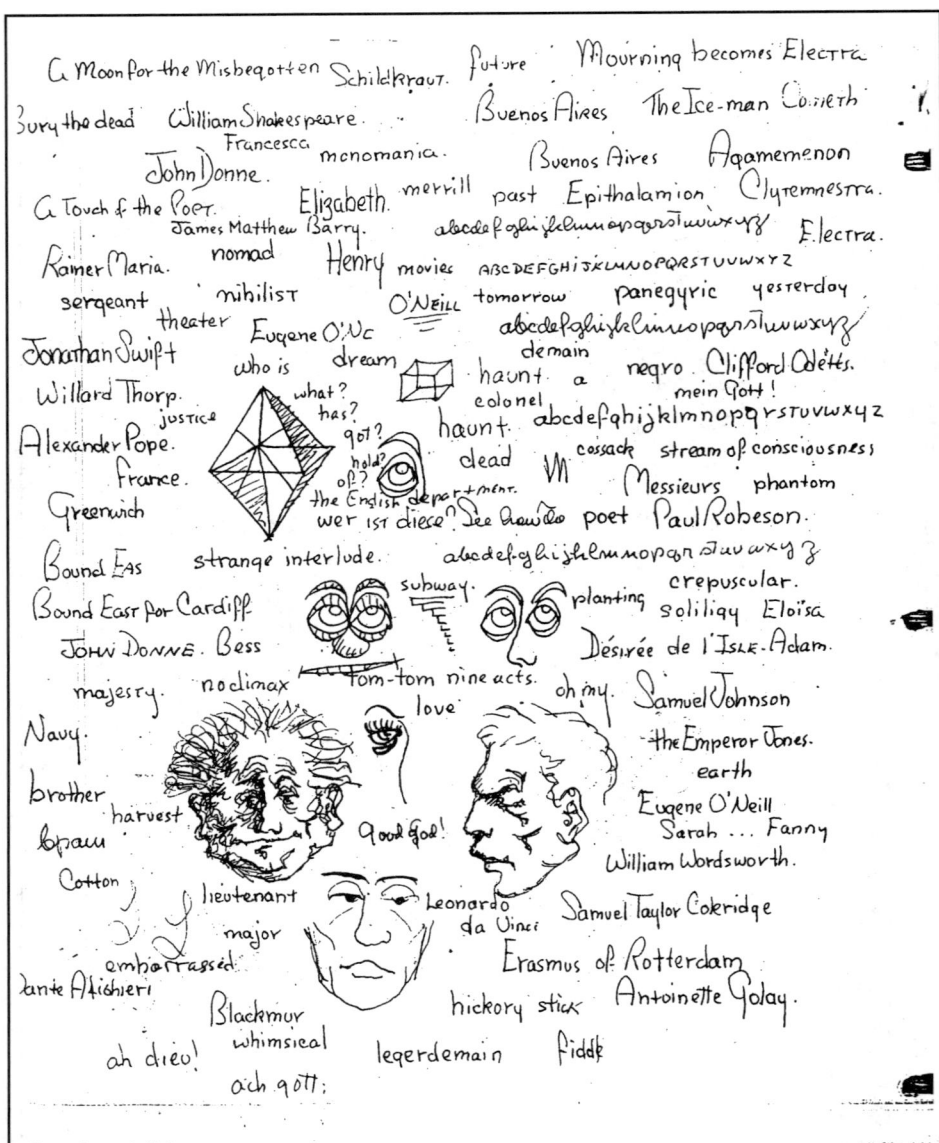

An Early Alphabet of Grace

Buechner Collection, Buswell Memorial Library, Wheaton College (IL)

ANGER

Of the Seven Deadly Sins, anger is possibly the most fun. To lick your wounds, to smack your lips over grievances long past, to roll over your tongue the prospect of bitter confrontations still to come, to savor to the last toothsome morsel both the pain you are given and the pain you are giving back—in many ways it is a feast fit for a king. The chief drawback is that what you are wolfing down is yourself. The skeleton at the feast is you.

Wishful Thinking: A Seeker's ABC

PSYCHOTHERAPY

After Adam and Eve ate the forbidden fruit, God came strolling through the cool of the day and asked them two questions: "Where are you?" and "What is this that you have done?" Psychotherapists, psychologists, psychiatrists, and the like have been asking the same ones ever since.

Whistling in the Dark: A Doubter's Dictionary

THE FALSE SELF

Life batters and shapes us in all sorts of ways before it's done . . .. The original, shimmering self gets buried so deep that most of us hardly end up living out of it at all. Instead, we live out all the other selves which we are constantly putting on and taking off like coats and hats against the world's weather.

Telling Secrets

Contents

Acknowledgments xi

Introduction xiii

Chapter 1
Buechner's Psychological-Spiritual Paradigm 1

Chapter 2
Listening to His Life: The Memoirs 25

Chapter 3
The Early Novels: Where Dreams Come From 51

Chapter 4
The Book of Bebb:
Psychology and Spirituality Personified 77

Chapter 5
Godric: A Medieval Saint Remembers 109

Chapter 6
The Son of Laughter: Healing the Shame that Binds 143

Appendix to Chapter 6
Jacob's Identity in the Christian and Literary Worlds 173

Chapter 7
Buechner's Psychological
Spirituality in a Postmodern World 179

Fiction by Frederick Buechner 187

Non-Fiction by Frederick Buechner 189

Works Cited 191

Acknowledgments

My heartfelt thanks to Mr. Buechner for his encouraging words during the research and writing of this book. I am grateful to the fine staff of the Archives and Special Collections of the Buswell Memorial Library at Wheaton College who helped me access their marvelous collection of Buechner papers. I also wish to thank the community of scholars at the Catholic University of America for creating a caring and stimulating academic environment which led to the successful completion of the dissertation on which this book is based. Special thanks to Professors Suarez, Winslow, Sendry, Damiani, and O'Connor, for their valuable insights and suggestions. Further appreciation goes to Chad Engbers, now teaching at Calvin College, for sharing Buechner enthusiasm and the practical realities of writing the dissertation, and to Shelly Harary for computer sanity. Finally, I extend my deepest thanks to my husband David for his inspiration, insight, and encouragement, and to our children, Marie and David, for their enthusiastic support.

Victoria Allen
Nassau, Bahamas
September 29, 2001

Introduction

In 1982 I became acquainted with the writings of Frederick Buechner through the moving pages of his first memoir *The Sacred Journey*. As the bookbuyer for the new Logos Bookstore in Nassau, Bahamas, I ordered the book at the suggestion of the Logos Association. Intrigued by the title, I began to read the slim volume and was immediately captured by the poetic insight Buechner brought to this memoir of his early life. He described his life "before time" as an age of innocence, when like Adam, he learned to name the animals and experienced a child's sensory immediacy and wonder, not unlike that described by James Joyce in *A Portrait of the Artist as a Young Man*. I was struck by Buechner's rude awakening "once upon a time" when as a ten-year-old he looked down from the upstairs window to view the motionless body of his father who had just committed suicide. And I was moved by his spiritual awakening to a dimension "beyond time" which changed the course of his life forever.

As I read and reread *The Sacred Journey*, Buechner's style reminded me of C.S. Lewis, whose *Chronicles of Narnia* I was reading to my children at the time. Like Lewis, Buechner's seemingly simple narrative revealed an unfolding spirituality of biblical proportions. At the same time, his deep psychological insight into his own motivation and experience echoed that of author/psychiatrist Dr. Paul Tournier.

The Sacred Journey provided my introduction to Frederick Buechner, but it was not until 1997, when as a doctoral candidate at The Catholic University of America I was searching for a topic for my dissertation, that I came to know his work on a deeper level. As a graduate student in English at Georgetown University, I had written my master's thesis on Flannery O'Connor. Now I was searching for an American author less analyzed by scholars, who also infused skilled literary expression with spiritual insight and a Christian worldview. When two fellow graduate students recommended Frederick Buechner, I learned that in addition to his memoirs he had written sixteen novels and numerous works of non-fiction. As I read the Buechner corpus, I began to see that Buechner's psychological/spiritual perspective in *The Sacred Journey* characterized his fiction. Not strange, for Buechner's creativity, psychological insights, and faith flow from a "deep inner place" (Brown 44), the *imago dei* where he sees with the eyes of the heart.

This book is an analysis of that creative spiritual and psychological interaction in the writings of Frederick Buechner. Drawing on psychological principles developed by Freud, Jung, Mahler and Kohut, the first chapter presents a paradigm for the integration of psychology and spiritually developed by Dr. David Allen.[1] Using Allen's paradigm of exploring the hurt trail, the false self (defenses, addictions), self-awareness (listening to your life), forgiveness and transcendence are discussed in terms of psychotherapeutic principles and human development.

The second chapter draws on Buechner's essays, lectures and three autobiographies to provide background from his non-fiction to illustrate his articulation of psychological and spiritual issues. The concept of "listening to your life," intrinsic to Buechner's approach, is the heart of the psychotherapeutic process stemming from Freud's emphasis on psychoanalytic listening. Seeing a spiritual connection to psychotherapy, Buechner cites God's questions to Adam and Eve in Genesis 3, "Where are you?" and "What is this that you have done?" and comments, "Psychotherapists, psychologists, psychiatrists, and the like have been asking the same ones ever since" (WD 105).

The third chapter introduces the earlier Buechner novels (written between 1950 and 1970), showing how these works contain psychological and spiritual concerns which prefigure his later development as a novelist. *The Final Beast* (1965), for example, introduces a therapist, modeled after the Episcopalian lay leader Agnes Sanford, who prays for the healing of her clients' memories, and who instructs the protagonist, a parish minister, to go beyond the secular psychological approach to fulfill his sacred role as priest/confessor.

The three subsequent chapters deal with three later novels, each unique but sharing common characteristics of the protagonist's quest for holiness, wholeness, and meaning. Chapter four explores *The Book of Bebb* (1979), a four-part modernist novel, told in the first person by a skeptical agnostic narrator who confronts Leo Bebb, a charismatic Southern preacher. Defenses, shame and guilt in both characters are exposed as the mystery of Bebb's past unfolds illustrating the concept of wounded healer. Psychological and spiritual approaches to listening to one's life are contrasted in the two main characters.

Buechner recasts a very different genre, medieval hagiography, in *Godric* (1980) to subvert the traditional view of holiness, the focus of chapter five. Based on the life of twelfth-century English saint Godric of Finchale, the ambivalence of spirituality, like psychological health, is portrayed as paradox. Narrated in the first person, as a confession of sorts, even Godric's speech is simultaneously sacred and profane, with the psychological/spiritual role of memory the dynamic Godric uses to listen to his life.

Son of Laughter (1993), the subject of chapter six, presents the Jacob narratives of Genesis from the autobiographical viewpoint of Jacob, the Hebrew patriarch, as he listens to his life. Plagued by toxic shame, Buechner's protagonist finds psychological and spiritual healing when he is changed from Jacob to Israel. Providing the character with psychological motivation, Buechner illustrates "the seemingly unrelated mysteries of human character and ultimate ideas" (Dillard A15).

The final chapter summarizes Buechner's significance as a novelist in bringing together spirituality and psychology. Joining writers such as Graham Greene, Walker Percy and Flannery O'Connor, who wove spiritual themes and religious insights into the fabric of the modern American novel, Buechner's integration of spirituality and psychology provides an original and particularly relevant contribution to postmodern American fiction.

As the twenty-first century dawns, theology has moved toward an appreciation of the personal and personal experience. Dynamics of contemporary Christian spirituality and pastoral theology in the works of Henri Nouwen (*The Wounded Healer,* 1979) are echoed in the behavioral sciences by psychiatrists such as Paul Tournier (*Guilt and Grace,* 1962), M. Scott Peck (*The Road Less Traveled: A New Psychology of Love, Traditional Values, and Spiritual Growth,* 1978), Gerald G. May (*Will and Spirit: A Contemplative Psychology,* 1982), Karl Menninger (*What Ever Happened to Sin?* 1988), Jeffrey H. Boyd (*Reclaiming the Soul,* 1996), David F. Allen (*In Search of the Heart,* 1993), and others who describe psychological principles of human behavior within the context of a Christian perspective. The recent narrative theology movement, which James Woeful calls the narrative-incarnational mode of theologizing (290)[2], similarly focuses on the importance of personal story to vitalize theological concepts. At the same time, the hermeneutical role of psychology in the study of autobiography brought to prominence by Eric Erickson in *Young Man Luther* (1958) views religious biography through a psychological lens.

Bridging the fields of psychology and theology, these writers underscore the personal and experiential nature of spiritual life with tools developed in the behavioral sciences. In contemporary American fiction, this interaction of psychological dynamics and spirituality is more creatively expressed in the works of Frederick Buechner than in any other writer. Judging from the enthusiastic response to my seminars on Buechner held at the Chautauqua Institution in New York, the many times he is quoted from the pulpit in churches across America, and the praise he has received from theologically innovative writers such as Philip Yancy, a growing number of readers are recognizing Buechner's contribution to American letters and Christian thought.

Buechner has made a unique contribution in the area of contemporary American fiction, an achievement all the more significant because he so intuitively expresses through literature developments within contemporary psychology and Christian spirituality. With particular focus on three of the later novels, *The Book of Bebb*, *Godric*, and *The Son of Laughter*, I wish to examine the ways Buechner employs psychological principles to convey spiritual insights. Whether focusing on a charismatic Southern preacher, a medieval saint, or an Old Testament patriarch, he integrates enlightened self analysis, psychologically revealing dreams, and literal and metaphorical exposures of past memories and shame in his characters' lives to demonstrate the dynamics of Christian faith seen through the lens of a psychologically-informed spirituality. By highlighting his effective use of psychological dynamics to convey spiritual realities, I wish to demonstrate Buechner's quality as a novelist and his relevance to a contemporary audience.

Notes

[1] Dr. David F. Allen trained in medicine at St. Andrews University, Scotland, and psychiatry at Harvard Medical School. He is board certified in Psychiatry and Addictions and has published five books in the areas of psychology and faith, human growth and mental health, drug addiction and treatment, as well as medical articles in the *Lancet* and *The Journal of Religion and Health*. In 1994 he founded The Renascence Clinic, a private psychiatric practice in Arlington, Virginia.

[2] See John Shea, *Stories of God: An Unauthorized Biography* (Chicago: Thomas More Press, 1978) and William J. Bausch, *Storytelling: Imagination and Faith* (Mystic, CT: Twenty-third Publications, 1984).

1

Buechner's Psychological-Spiritual Paradigm

PSYCHOTHERAPY

After Adam and Eve ate the forbidden fruit, God came strolling through the cool of the day and asked them two questions: "Where are you?" and "What is this that you have done?" Psychotherapists, psychologists, psychiatrists, and the like have been asking the same ones ever since.

"Where are you?" lays bare the present. They are in hiding, that's where they are. What is it they want to hide? From whom do they want to hide it? What does it cost them to hide it? Why are they so unhappy with things as they are that they are trying to conceal it from the world by hiding, and from themselves by covering, their nakedness with aprons?

"What is this that you have done?" lays bare the past. What did they do to get this way? What did they hope would happen by doing it? What did they fear would happen? What did the serpent do? What was it that made them so ashamed?

God is described as cursing them then, but in view of his actions at the end of the story and right on through the end of the New Testament, it seems less a matter of vindictively inflicting them with the consequences than of honestly confronting them with the consequences. Because of who they are and what they have done, this is the result. There is no undoing it. There is no going back to the garden.

But then comes the end of the story where God with his own hands makes them garments of skins and clothes them. It is the most moving part of the story. They can't go back, but they can go forward clothed in a new way—clothed, that is, not in the sense of having their old defenses again behind which to hide who they are and what they have done but in the sense of having a new understanding of who they are and a new strength to draw on for what lies before them to do now.

Many therapists wouldn't touch biblical teachings with a ten-foot pole, but in their own way, and at their best, they are often following them. (WD 105-106)

In his thought-provoking lexicon *Whistling in the Dark: A Doubter's Dictionary* (1988), Frederick Buechner demonstrates the interrelatedness of psychology and Christian spirituality by casting the interaction between God and the first humans in Genesis 3 as a psychotherapy session. God, in the role of therapist, asks probing questions to encourage his patients to face their unconscious (hidden) conflicts. These questions involve reality testing of the present and psychotherapeutic probing of the past to bring understanding to the present. Buechner uses the narrative details from Genesis 3, the physical hiding of Adam and Eve, the shame at literal nakedness, the attempts at covering, as metaphors of psychological-spiritual states: hiding the real self, using defense mechanisms to deal with shame and guilt resulting in alienation and isolation. In contrast, God's therapeutic intervention allows humans to confront reality, gain insights and receive healing.

Buechner's psychological-spiritual paradigm underscores the importance of his recurrent theme: listen to your life. Whether in his autobiographies, sermons, lectures or novels, listening to your life, a form of self-analysis, is the process leading to understanding truths about the self and God. God, the originator of psychotherapy, is ever present, seeking to guide and direct. But for the therapy to work, the patient must be willing to become engaged in the therapeutic process by actively listening to the past and present of his or her own life.

Buechner's claim, that many therapists "wouldn't touch biblical teachings with a ten-foot pole, but in their own way, and at their best, they are often following them" is worth a more thorough examination. Although Sigmund Freud was an atheist who called religion "the universal obsessional neurosis" (*Totem and Taboo*), his concept of analytic listening, a method of investigating the mind fundamental to psychoanalytic psychology, is similar to the technique Buechner is applying to his concept of knowing God. According to Freud, free association, central to the methodology of classic psychoanalysis, provides the therapeutic situation for a temporary therapeutic regression, to enable patients to reexperienc suppressed memories from the painful past. Once these past experiences become conscious, the patient may be guided in resolving them. In his or her interventions, the psychoanalyst is guided primarily by the manifestation of transference and resistance. Analytical interpretation is then used to gain insight and foster change in the patient's intrapsychic balance.

As the father of psychiatry, Freud's insights have helped shape the overall "psyche" of the twentieth century, as such ubiquitous

Freudian terminology attests. More specifically, Freudian techniques form the basis of most psychotherapy, and psychoanalytically oriented psychotherapy is the most widely practiced form of psychotherapy in the United States (Inderbitzin and James 138). Insight oriented (expressive) psychotherapy and supportive psychotherapy are not dichotomous methods of treatment. As in Buechner's illustration of the Creator's probing questions in Genesis 3, the goal of the therapist's questions is to allow the patient to see his condition in a new light. Whether through free association (psychoanalysis) or through more directive psychotherapy, the therapist elicits from the patient the unconscious conflicts stemming from childhood. The relationship between the patient and the therapist allows the patient to expose himself, or as in Buechner's application of the Genesis model, to face his nakedness.

Despite his insistence on the neutrality of the therapist, Freud considered positive transference necessary and useful in the patient's relationship to the analyst. This allowed the patient to unconsciously apply feelings, attitudes, and expectations from important persons in the past to the therapist. From experiences as a young child with parents, the patient would then transfer dependent, sexual, and aggressive feelings and wishes to the therapist. The therapist then draws connections between the patient's present experience (associations, dreams, or fears) and his underlying unconscious conflicts or patterns of thought.

Buechner's theme is that in listening to one's life, one will begin to catch sight of the patterns moving beneath the surface where God is present. Even if not fully understood or accepted, as one listens, a sense of God's presence and a relationship, like the psychiatrist's therapeutic treatment alliance, will develop. Listening to one's life involves asking questions and listening for answers. It also involves hearing the questions being asked. Thus the basis of Buechner's approach to spiritual growth parallels psychoanalysis in its method of investigation, although, like post Freudians, he does not see the role of the therapist as neutral.

In addition to its method of investigation, Buechner's approach to spirituality rests on seeking underlying meanings, the mental interconnectedness of past and present experience. This resembles the basic assumption of psychoanalysis, that

> all psychological events are determined by antecedent ones and . . . nothing occurs by chance in mental life. The unconscious or topographic point of view, like psychic determinism, is so well established that these two hypotheses have been described as established laws of the mind (Inderbitzin and James 109).

The "Freudian slip" is one such unconscious revelation of interconnectedness. Since Buechner's concept of personal development contains many psychoanlytical elements, the importance of listening to one's life to understand, if only in retrospect, its unfolding story cannot be overestimated.

In 1923 Freud developed his structural model of the unconscious, seeing unconscious mental behavior in terms of the id (source of motivation and instinctual drives directed by the pleasure principle), the superego (which functions as the conscience providing moral values, standards, and prohibitions), and the ego (which embodies the goals and aspirations of the person, regulates self-esteem, and protects the self against narcissistic injury). Through complex defense mechanisms, such as repression, identification, isolation of affect, reaction formation, regression, projection, reversal, turning against the self, and sublimation (Anna Freud, *The Ego and Mechanisms of Defense*, 1936), the ego draws on involuntary, unconscious psychological activities in response to signals of anxiety or other unpleasurable feelings such as depression, guilt, or shame.

Buechner subscribes to a similar viewpoint based on his personal experience in psychotherapy, which his characters who actively listen to their lives discover. Freud's analysis of Hamlet's

Oedipal complex or Lacan's psychoanalytic literary interpretations usually view literature like life in terms of underlying obsessions and conflicts which are primarily sexual. In Buechner's writings, tapping into the unconscious often reveals levels of reality which are psychological or spiritual. Thus dreams, unconscious connections, hunches, even "Freudian slips" are extremely significant in providing clues as to a character's past and present in far more than a sexual context. The Christian belief in a transcendent, yet personal deity, manifested Incarnate at a point in history and continuing to interact with creation through the power of the Holy Spirit, adds a spiritual dimension to the concept of listening to one's life.

According to Buechner, like an author, the benevolent creator mysteriously reveals his love through an alphabet of grace which can be discerned as one listens to the story of one's life. In his lexicon *Whistling in the Dark,* Buechner connects Christian doctrine with personal experience as he explores the meaning of the word "story":

STORY

It is well to remember what the ancient creeds of the Christian faith declare credence in.

God of God, Light of Light . . . for us and for our salvation came down from heaven . . . born of the Virgin Mary . . . suffered . . . crucified . . . dead . . . buried . . . . rose again . . . sitteth on the right hand of God . . . shall come again, with glory, to judge both the quick and the dead. That is not a theological idea of a religious system. It is a series of largely flesh and blood events that happened, are happening, will happen, in time and space. For better or worse, it is a story. . . . the Truth that Christianity claims to be true is ultimately to be found, if it's to be found at all, not in the Bible, or the Church, or

> Theology—the best they can do is point to the Truth—but in our own stories.
>
> If the God you believe in as an idea doesn't start showing up in what happens to you in your own life, you have as much cause for concern as if the God you don't believe in as an idea does start to show up.
>
> It is absolutely crucial, therefore, to keep in constant touch with what is going on in your own life's story and to pay close attention to what is going on in the stories of others' lives. If God is present anywhere, it is in those stories that God is present. If God is not present in those stories, then you might as well give up the whole business. (WD 114-115)

As a storyteller, Buechner gives spiritual realities concrete expression in his novels. In the article "Frederick Buechner: The Novelist as Theologian," James Woelfel praises Buechner's literary skill as a storyteller to bring alive theological insight:

> Of particular value in Buechner's contribution is that he comes to theological reflection primarily as a talented literary artist and storyteller, with the singular perspective his craft brings to bear on the relations among experience, language, imagination, and thought. Equally important is the fact that Buechner is a working embodiment, in both his fictional and his autobiographical writings, of precisely that narrative-incarnational mode of theologizing that is being talked about so much today by its theoreticians. (290)

Describing Buechner's application of "the relations among experience, language, imagination, and thought" to theology is similar to saying Buechner uses psychological techniques to express spiritual realities. As a novelist, speaking through characterization, he uses words, thoughts, emotions, and actions to express psychological and spiritual concepts. One must listen between the lines to understand the use of imagery, symbol, and setting, and discern implications of character and plot in order to hear the theme of the story. Similarly, one must listen to one's own life.

In his personal life, Buechner has found psychotherapy an important way to listen to his life as indicated in his last memoir *Telling Secrets*. Coming to terms with his father's suicide, growing in his relationship with his family, and understanding himself have required professional help for insight and healing. In this sense, Buechner's view of "listening to his life" for the alphabet of grace has taken a psychologically informed direction which enhances rather than contradicts spiritual understanding. Since Freud and Jung have so imprinted contemporary psychology, to present their influence on psychotherapy serves as a way to speak about this amorphous field.

Despite his disparate perspective on the existence of God, Freud's views of the experience of life, especially life without divine grace, can be understood in Christian terms. According to psychiatrist Armand Nicholi, Freud felt the human condition was wounded:

> Life as we find it is too hard for us; it brings us too many pains, disappointments, and impossible tasks. . . . We are threatened with suffering from three directions: from our own body, which is doomed to decay . . .from the external world which may rage against us with overwhelming and merciless forces of destruction. . . . We are threatened with suffering from our relationships to other men. The suffering which comes from this last source is perhaps more painful to us than any other. (112)

To protect itself from this overwhelming sense of hopelessness, the human psyche uses defenses, "palliative measures—distractions, intoxicants, or denial" (112). Indeed, Freud may not have "touched biblical teaching with a ten foot pole," due to his own hurt trail.

In addition, James W. Jones, author of *Contemporary Psychoanalysis and Religion: Transference and Transcendence,* explains Freud's religious antagonism in its historical context:

> An heir of the Enlightenment, Freud assumed that atheism was normative and religion was but a vestige of the childhood of humankind. Psychoanalysis was to complete the Comptian [sic] project of the vanquishing of religion by science, extending the hegemony of Newtonian mechanism and Darwinian naturalism into the depths of the soul. The sublimest ecstasies and the most profound sensibilities were to be broken down into their instinctual components and the mechanics of lust and aggression. (1)

Within this perspective, Freud explained away the rise of religion from causes ranging from pathology to wish fulfillment. In *Totem and Taboo* he diagnosed religion as an "obsessional neurosis . . . an attempt to ward off oedipal guilt through obsessive repetition of ritual and reconciliation to an idealized patriarchal father god" (Jones 2). In *The Future of an Illusion* Freud explained the rise of religion as a primitive, childlike wish to preserve the safety of parental protection: "Through fantasy, religion reduces the terror of an uncaring nature by personalizing the natural order, removes the fear of death by providing an illusion of immortality, and reconciles us to the social necessity of self-denial by promising to reward us for it in the hereafter" (Jones 2).

Thus "God was but a projection of the childish wish for an all-powerful father who would protect one from the unpredictable, harsh elements of nature" (Nicholi 113). Psychoanalysis, which Freud called an "education to reality"

> would render religion implausible and unnecessary.... Taught the rational importance of self-control, civilized people would no longer require pious authoritarianism. Health would require renouncing the wondrous but unattainable wishes of childhood for the realistic but prosaic satisfactions of adulthood. (Jones 3)

In his fiction, Buechner uses Freud's anti-religious perspective in creating Antonio Parr, the skeptical narrator of *The Book of Bebb* whom he pits against his most religious protagonist, Leo Bebb. The psychologically oriented narrator and the religious fanatic seem poles apart until Buechner's psychological spirituality begins to bring them together. As Bebb's psychological weaknesses become apparent, so do Parr's spiritual needs and his growing awareness that the events of his life may not be random happenstance. Thus Buechner skillfully employs Freudian concepts as sometimes contradictory and sometimes complementary to a spiritual perspective.

In spite of Freud's public optimism concerning the potential of the human race, freed from childish superstition and enlightened by psychoanalysis as expressed in *The Future of an Illusion*, his private view of human nature could well be described as "fallen," as is apparent from his candid writings to Oskar Pfister: "I have found little that is good about human beings on the whole. In my experience most of them are trash no matter whether they publicly subscribe to this or that ethical doctrine or to none at all" (Meng and Freud 61). Buechner's view of human beings is far more charitable, for although he underscores the "fair/foul" duality in his most heroic characters, even his most pitiful are valuable as persons, and God's grace is present when they expose their need. Thus Buechner uses Freudian psychology when it applies, as in the concept of transference to the presence of an all-loving God and the value of psychoanalytical listening with a therapist to expose painful memories and to see moments of grace. He satirizes Freudian reductionism in the all-knowing quips of Antonio Parr, who begins by using Freudian interpretations as a defense against genuine spirituality and honest self-analysis.

If Freud sought to replace religion with psychoanalysis, Carl Jung "sought its transformation into a universal form of wisdom" (Jones 3). Whereas Freud's theory of libido reduced behavior to biological drives, Jung saw the psyche's driving force (libido) as undifferentiated psychic energy which could go in positive and negative directions. For Jung the basic psychological drive was not instinctual, biological gratification but psychological and spiritual integration through a process he called individuation. "Neurosis arises not from repressed instincts but from split off parts of the self . . . 'complexes'—parts split off and repressed because they do not fit with our image of ourselves or the persona that our culture reinforces" (Jones 4). The task of analysis is to help the psyche integrate its repressed or split off sides. Due to the shared collective unconscious, images and themes expressed as archetypes, individuation involved "the recovery not simply of suppressed parts of our personality but also of the universal aspects of human nature" (Jones 4).

According to Jung, religion used to provide access to these important archetypal patterns of human experience, and thus enabled individuation. With the decline of religion, Jungian analysis was needed to aid in the recovery of the spiritual center underlying the psyche. Thus,

> the task of Jungian analysis was not just the cure of personal neurosis but also the recovery of the sacred buried within each self. In pursuit of this goal, Jung's psychology became a theology in disguise—envisioning a universal power outside of conscious control that brings health and

wholeness when accessed through dream, symbol, and intuitive experience. (Jones 5)

In Buechner's novels, Jungian archetypes are used to amplify the spiritual significance of imagery and events. In his first novel, *A Long Day's Dying*, archetypal religious symbols of priest, unicorn, and birds from the Philomela myth provide an ambivalent quality of unsubstantial spirituality which is more form than substance. Later in *The Book of Bebb* Buechner weaves in mythological references to Orpheus' and Dante's descents to the underworld to parallel becoming aware of the psychological and spiritual issues going on beneath the surface of existence.

Jung's emphasis on the spiritual archetypal center is used by Buechner to underscore the importance of listening to one's life, of keeping one's spiritual eyes and ears open to discern the alphabet of grace which is ever present but often overlooked. Buechner also attributes directly to Jung his understanding of the presence of God, whether or not one is aware of it, which is a reoccurring theme of *Alphabet of Grace* and most of his later novels Summarizing the things he would be willing to "bet maybe even my life on," Buechner states:

> That—as I picked up somewhere in Jung and whittled into the ash stick I use for tramping around through the woods sometimes—*vocatus atque non vocatus Deus aderit*, which I take to mean that in the long run, whether you call on him or don't call on him, God will be present with you. That if we really had our eyes open, we would see that all moments are key moments. (NT 108)

In addition to insights from Freud and Jung, psychological paradigms have come to include the interrelatedness of the self to other selves. Contemporary approaches to personality theory tend to focus on interpersonal relationships rather than seeing the individual as a separate and self-contained system of instinctual or archetypal forces. Thus in addition to Freudian and Jungian emphasis on the individual, internalized patterns of interpersonal behavior are the focus of analysis in developmental object relations theory and self psychology (Heinz Kohut), family therapy, and recovery models (e.g., Alcoholics Anonymous) from the 1970s.

Material for the psychological issues faced by Jacob in *The Son of Laughter* reflects these interpersonal therapeutic concerns. Jacob's toxic shame and dysfunctional family are amplified by Buechner in his novel. Healing depends on a combination of spiritual forgiveness and psychotherapeutic transference to a loving Father God. Jacob's relationship to his family begins with dysfunctional codependency on his mother and shameful disregard for his father. After Jacob is freed from his bondage of shame, he assumes his calling and accepts responsibility when faced by problems with his own sons. Moving from shameful isolation, Jacob becomes a patriarch with the Fear's blessing. Heinz Kohut's statement "A self can never exist outside a matrix of selfobjects" (Jones 17) applies to Jacob's psychological and spiritual experience. Selfobjects are those relationships through which we "maintain the cohesion, vitality, strength, and harmony of the self" (17), relationships creating a strong sense of self in the child. The child thus absorbs the affective quality and patterns of relatedness of the relationship with the parents, but throughout adult life, according to Kohut, he or she continues to be influenced by selfobject relations. Thus in contrast to the Freudian concept of immature transference which the healthy person outgrows, Kohut's object relations theory sees transference as ongoing throughout life and more fully developed as the person's "need to experience mirroring and acceptance, his need to experience merger with greatness, strength and calmness; and his need to experience the presence of essential alikeness" (18).

Kohut's three essential transference needs for the development of a healthy self parallel Buechner's psychological and spiritual approach to listening to life. The idealizing transference, connecting the self with a greater, ideal reality, reflects the concept of the Creator God who made humans in his own image (*imago dei*), and whose consciousness contains a God-shaped vacuum which can only be filled by God the creator. Kohut's mirroring transference, the need for recognition and acceptance, parallels the Christian view of the loving Father-God. Buechner's Genesis definition of psychotherapy emphasizes the Creator who seeks out his wayward creatures, provides for them with covering, and ultimately in the New Testament so loved the world that He sent his only Son to redeem it (John 3:16). Kohut's twinship transference, the need to experience that others are like us, finds parallels in the concept of being part of the family of God, joint heirs with Christ, and fellow heirs of the promise of God with other believers. Leo Bebb's Princeton love feasts reflect twinship transference, as does the loyal community Bebb always has around him. Rephrased, this is the heart of the Christian message: God first loved humankind. Therefore humans are to love God and their neighbors as themselves. Although writing from a purely psychiatric, secular perspective, Kohut's observations significantly modify Freud's concept of transference in ways which may parallel transcendent religious faith, rather than dismiss it as neurosis or wish fulfillment.

Buechner's concept of listening to your life has many parallels with psychotherapy. The goal of psychoanalytic understanding, according to Stolorow, Lachmann and Atwood, is to bring out "the structure, significance, origins, and therapeutic transformations of personal subjective worlds in all their richness and diversity" (Jones 24). The interpersonal dialogue with a therapist is designed to illuminate the inner patterns of the person's life, the underlying structures of meaning outwardly expressed in ideas, wishes, fears and behaviors, very much like the patterns revealed in listening to one's life. As in Kohut's object relations theory, the quality needed in the therapist is not supposed neutrality but empathy, an understanding and entering into the patient's world from the heart. Transference, the forming of a working therapeutic alliance between client and therapist, fosters the reworking and healing of the client's sense of self.

This shift from an emphasis on the isolated individual to interpersonal, interactional relationships characterizes self psychology and family therapy, the "two most powerful psychological theories of the second half of [the 20th] century" (Jones 28). This shift is also reflected in the psychological approach of Frederick Buechner.

Since "transference is the major category in which psychotherapeutic change is understood psychoanalytically" (Jones 86), Buechner's concept of listening to your life may be seen as the enactment of a transference relationship between the person and God. If transference in psychological terms promotes psychotherapeutic health, it may even, as Jones contends, apply to religious transformation. How then do contemporary therapists describe the workings of transference?

In terms of the earliest "transference" or relationship between mother and child, the work of Margaret Mahler is fundamental and widely accepted. Mahler's separation/individuation model describes the ideal relationship of the infant to the mother as changing developmentally from fusion to rapprochement to consolidation and object constancy to a gradual integration of the image of the mother as reliable and stable within the child, even when the mother is not physically present. Building on Mahler's model, James Masterson states the "caregiver's mirroring is the most important ingredient in the development of the sense of self" (24). If this significant interaction between mother (caregiver) and child is missing, the child experiences the "abandonment depression," involving "depression, guilt, helplessness and hopelessness, and massive rage" (40). To defend against emotional pain, the child erects "defensive self-representations" or a "false self", to protect the inner "real self." Therapy seeks to uncover the inner hurt self by working through defenses, supporting the client in reexperiencing original painful experiences, and finding in the therapeutic relationship a safe place for the real self to develop.

Different therapeutic models have different methods and goals, but they all focus on the relationship between client and therapist as a way to move beyond the false self, to restore the inner real self to healthy functioning and interpersonal relationships.

Though some secular therapists wouldn't touch biblical teaching with a ten-foot pole, therapists consciously working within a Judeo-Christian perspective have integrated aspects of psychological theory and biblical teaching.[1] Christian spirituality in the works of Catholic writers Henry Nouwen, William H. Shannon, Thomas Keating, and Thomas Merton have made Christian teaching on contemplative prayer accessible to many psychologists and laypersons who seek to integrate psychological and spiritual growth and renewal.

Using the term "false self" articulated by Thomas Merton and others from the writings of Bernard of Clairveaux, psychiatrist Dr. David Allen speaks about the "hurt trail" resulting from the wounded condition of human existence. Although made in the image of God, humans are wounded, alienated from the creator and living in a fallen world where they experience a sense of change, loss, and pain. To cope with the pain of life, humans develop a protective "false self" to cope with the emotional trauma in early childhood and to defend against psychological pain throughout life. As in the work of Masterson, Kohut, and Winnicott, the concept of the false self has long been used by spiritual writers who are familiar with the concept from personal experience.

The Trappist monk and writer Thomas Merton describes "an illusory person: a false self" (*Seeds of Contemplation* 28), a term which he borrowed from the writings of the fourteenth-century monk Bernard of Clairveaux. As Merton explains:

> After all, what is your personal identity? It is what you really are, your real self. None of us is what he thinks he is, or what other people think he is, still less what his passport says he is. Many of us think no doubt, that we are what we would

like to be. And it is fortunate for most of us that we are mistaken. We do not generally know what is good for us. That is because, in St. Bernard's language, our true personality has been concealed under the "disguise" of a false self, the ego whom we tend to worship in place of God. (*The Waters of Siloe* 349)

Thomas Keating, a Cistercian monk and founder of the Centering Prayer movement, has written numerous books on spirituality and contemplative prayer. In *Open Mind, Open Heart*, he defines the false self as "the self developed in our own likeness rather than in the likeness of God; the self-image developed to cope with the emotional trauma of early childhood, which seeks happiness by satisfying the instinctual needs of survival/security, affection/esteem, and power/control and bases its self-worth on cultural or group identification" (146). In order to communicate to contemporary readers in the Western world, Keating describes the psychology of Centering Prayer as "Divine Therapy" because, "Therapy suggests a climate of friendship and the trust that a topnotch therapist is able to inspire, while at the same time emphasizing that we come to therapy with a variety of serious emotional and mental problems" (*Intimacy with God* 72).

Like Buechner's description of Adam and Eve's aprons, according to Allen the false self is fashioned as a defense against nakedness and vulnerability, but it also blocks oneness with God, self, and others. From the false self develop multiple defenses such as projections, prejudices, preoccupation, withdrawal, fantasy, exaltation of self (arrogance, pride) or abasement of self (deprecation, despair), lying, narcissism. However, the false self is a perverse rescuer. In seeking to provide a coping mechanism to defend against hurt and pain and prevent insecurity, low self esteem, fear of abandonment, and feeling of being out of control, the false self actually blocks meaning, creativity, and love, and becomes in fact an internal saboteur, promising life but delivering soul death.

Like the secular therapists, Allen stresses the importance of analysis or psychotherapy to bring subconscious conflicts to the surface where they can be resolved. Reparenting the wounded child may also be an aspect of therapy, although the transcendent dimension of faith, hope, and love is a departure from traditional analysis. Intrinsic to Christian therapy is the need to focus on past hurts, disappointments and shameful experiences (the hurt trail). By working the hurt trail through specific exercises, as well as in therapeutic dialogue, the client not only comes to recognize past hurts but also may need to seek forgiveness and healing from God, from others, and from him or herself. Like Christian faith, Renascence therapy includes the need to give and receive forgiveness.

As described in Buechner's Genesis passage, the consequences of the Fall cannot be ignored. Original sin and a fallen human nature are the common experience of human beings and affect human behavior on many levels. Therapy thus begins with getting in touch with the past: the hurt trail.

In light of the Christian faith, however, God has intervened to make provision for his creatures. Despite their disfigurement, the fact that human beings are made in the image of God (*imago dei*) has not been totally obliterated, and does shine through beneath the false self. In addition, through his love, manifested in the incarnation of Jesus Christ and his sacrificial death, the benevolent God of the universe provides humankind with "a new understanding of who they are and a new strength to draw on for what lies before them to do now" (WD 106).

Thus, a major difference stemming from the Christian perspective is the belief that humans, though fallen, are made in the image of God (*imago dei*), and thus have inherent meaning, dignity, identity and value. As explained by Allen, because life is "wounded" or fallen, ego defenses cover up the real, hurt self, which though wounded still bears a reflection of and transference to God. God only deals with the real self, so by getting in touch with our real selves, we become open to receiving God's love and experiencing what Allen calls our love story. Thus Christ's words, I came for the sick, or the lost, or the sinners, applies to the hurt self. "I came not to call the righteous but sinners to repentance." It is only when the person admits woundedness that the love of God can be received. Through the process of dropping the false self, and its attachment to the pseudogods of the culture, the real self begins to emerge. As Allen states, "The surgeon may cut, the psychiatrist may listen, but only God's love heals."

Along the lines of Allen's description of the well-defended false self and the need to get in contact with the hurt wounded self, Buechner defines "help" in terms of his uncanny psychological-spiritual perspective:

Help

As they're used psychologically, words like repression, denial, sublimation, defense, all refer to one form or another of the way human beings erect walls to hide behind both from each other and from themselves. You repress the memory that is too painful to deal with, say. You deny your weight problem. You sublimate some of your sexual energy by channeling it into other forms of activity more socially acceptable. You conceal your sense of inadequacy behind a defensive bravado. And so on and so forth. The inner state you end up with is a castle-like affair to keep, inner wall, outer wall, moat, which you erect originally to be a fortress to keep the enemy out but which turns into a prison where you become the jailer and thus your own enemy. It is a wretched and lonely place. You can't be what you want to be there or do what you want to do. People can't see through all the masonry to who you truly are, and half the time you're not sure you can see who you truly are yourself, you've been walled up so long.

Fortunately there are two words that offer a way out, and they're simply these: Help me. It's not always easy to say them—you have your pride after all, and you're not sure there's anybody you trust enough to say them to—but they're always worth saying. To another human being—a friend, a stranger? To God? Maybe it comes to the same thing.

Help me. They open a door through the walls, that's all. At least hope is possible again. At least you're no longer alone. (WD 65-66)

Using his own metaphorical terminology, the fortified castle with the moat, Buechner has described the false self developed to cope with the hurt trail, or in Freudian terms, the ego and its defenses. He has also hinted at the remedy—a process of psychotherapy, with a professional, a friend, or with God—as a way to get help.

Listening to his life through his three memoirs, Buechner poignantly describes his hurt trail, which began as a child with his father's suicide, and led to his final recognition of his own need for professional psychotherapy. Rather than becoming a substitute for his faith in God, psychotherapy enhanced it as he came to understand his life in terms of God's therapeutic working in and through it. In other words, by examining his hurt trail he was able to experience the fullness of his love story.

For Buechner there is a mysterious connection between the inner self and the image of God, the psychological and the spiritual center deep within which is also the source of artistic creativity. As he explains:

> I believe there is within us this image of God, which is perhaps another way of saying it. Inner light is another. There is something deep within us, in everybody, that gets buried and distorted and confused and corrupted by what happens to us. But it is there as a source of insight and healing and strength. I think it's where art comes from. For instance, partly out of that inner place I've written things which were a tremendous help to me. *Godric* was one. At a time when I was in desperate need, out of that deep place came this holy old man about whom I knew nothing, and he became really for me a kind of saint. I can't explain it. The words were mine; I put every word he says into his mouth. It was my pen, but I was drawing on this deep source. Does this make any sense at all? (Brown interview in *Of Fiction and Faith* 44)

A connection between creative expression and the artist's unconscious exists as Buechner describes. However much more than tapping into one's psyche is involved in literary creativity, and interpretive literary readings based solely on psychological insights can be overly reductionistic. Critical scholar Frederick Crews explains how his own literary psychoanalysis of Hawthorne in *The Sins of the Fathers: Hawthorne's Psychological Themes* (1966) suffered from overzealous methodizing (*The Critics Bear It Away* 3-15). In terms of critical theories for reading literature, the New Critics looked askance at the "intentional fallacy,"[2] the error of interpreting literature in terms of the author's supposed intention, whether conscious or unconscious, rather than what was "objectively" in the work. Putting the intentional fallacy debate of the New Critics into perspective, M. H. Abrams states:

>   Reference to the author's supposed purposes or else to the author's personal situation and state of mind in writing a text, is held to be a harmful mistake, because it diverts our attention to such "external" matters as the author's biography, or psychological condition, or creative process, which we substitute for the proper critical concern with the "internal" constitution and inherent value of the literary product.
>
>   ... this claim, which was central in the New Criticism, has been strenuously debated, and has been reformulated by both of its original proponents. . . . A view acceptable to many traditional critics . . . is that in the exceptional instances—for example, in Henry James' prefaces to his novels—where we possess an author's express statement about his artistic intentions in a literary work, that statement should constitute evidence for an interpretive hypothesis, but should not in itself be determinative. (90)

The key is to find a balance between understanding the literary work by itself and through insights gained from the author's life. Many New Critical studies such as Brooks, Lewis, and Warren's *Makers and the Making* did include biographical sketches of writers as supplementary tools for the full comprehension of an author's work within the context of the times. When an author commented on his purposes, these comments were to be considered as long as they did not negate a reasonable reading. For example Henry James' prefaces, written after the initial publication of the works, are seen as valuable assets to understanding the writer's process. In Buechner's memoirs and interviews, we have a similar source, the author's reflections on his experience during the writing of his books. An author's biography, or psychological condition, or creative process is not a substitute for the literary analysis of his work, but they may provide a deeper appreciation and understanding of the fiction as a literary creation. Reflecting his changing perspective over the years, Buechner's comments on his own life support the hypothesis that he consciously and unconsciously uses psychotherapeutic insights to create his characters and to integrate realities of Christian experience in his fiction.

Notes

[1] See *Modern Psycho-Therapies: A Comprehensive Christian Appraisal*. Jones, Santon L. and Richard E. Butman. Downers Grove, IL: InterVarsity Press, 1991.

[2] The term used by W. K. Wimsatt and Monroe C. Beardsley was associated with interpretive errors in the New Criticism. See "The Intentional Fallacy" (1946) reprinted in Wimsatt's *The Verbal Icon* (1964).

2

Listening to His Life: The Memoirs

> Listen to your life. See it for the fathomless mystery that it is. In the boredom and pain of it no less than in the excitement and gladness: touch, taste, smell your way to the holy and hidden heart of it because in the last analysis all moments are key moments, and life itself is grace. What I started trying to do as a writer and as a preacher was more and more to draw on my own experience not just as a source of plot, character, illustration, but as a source of truth. (NT 87)

Buechner's first autobiographical journal *The Alphabet of Grace* expresses his major theme "listen to your life." Listening to life describes a way to hear the spiritual dimensions of one's life to sense the presence of God working through everyday reality. A few years later, Buechner came to include psychotherapy as a complementary way of listening to his life. Therapeutic analysis, guided by a skilled therapist, provided an analytical tool for listening to one's life. Thus the psychodynamic component of listening to one's life is central to Buechner's fully developed psychological-spiritual approach.

The initial process began when Buechner articulated his experience of listening to his life in the late 1960s. After nine years as chaplain at Phillips Exeter Academy, he moved with his family to Vermont to devote himself to writing and lecturing. He was having great difficulty completing his fifth novel, *The Entrance to Porlock*, when he received an invitation to give The William Belden Noble Lectures at Harvard in 1969. In response he wrote to ask for further clarification on the topic for these lectures to be presented in Memorial Church. Buechner relates the answer he received and its unexpected significance in his memoir *Now and Then*:

> Perhaps something in the area of "religion and letters," he wrote back, and it was the word *letters* that did it.
>
> What he meant by the word was clear enough, but suddenly I found myself thinking of letters literally instead—of letters as the alphabet itself, the A's, B's, C's and D's out of which all literature, all words, are ultimately composed. And from there I wandered somehow to the notion of the events of our lives—even, and perhaps especially, the most everyday events—as the alphabet through which God, of his grace, spells out his words, his meaning to us. So *The Alphabet of Grace* was the title I hit upon, and what I set out to do was to try to describe a single representative day of my life in a way to suggest what there was of God to hear in it . . .. In writing those lectures and the book they later turned into, it came to seem to me that if I were called upon to state in a few words the essence of everything I was trying to say both as a novelist and as a preacher, it would be something like this: Listen to your life.

> See it for the fathomless mystery that it is. In the boredom and pain of it no less than in the excitement and gladness: touch, taste, smell your way to the holy and hidden heart of it because in the last analysis all moments are key moments, and life itself is grace. What I started trying to do as a writer and as a preacher was more and more to draw on my own experience not just as a source of plot, character, illustration, but as a source of truth. (86-87)

For the lectures, Buechner wrote a first-person autobiographical journal describing the events in daily life and the ways God possibly speaks through them. Published as *The Alphabet of Grace* (1970), it recounts the rambling musings of the author as he examines his own life for one waking day. Interspersed are poetic descriptions of weather (mostly rain), quotes of poetry, philosophical comments, practical care for children, impressions of sights and sounds and thoughts as he pursues his daily routine. It is unguarded, combining flashbacks of his life and observations about how he is feeling about the past, present, and future and, most importantly, for the first time Buechner writes in the first person. Although he does not use the specific terminology in the lectures, we are witnessing the author listening to his life, a central theme in all Buechner's subsequent writings. *Alphabet of Grace* marks a definitive shift in Buechner's writing in theme and style which was to leave a lasting imprint on his subsequent work.

Several years later, after he was in therapy, Buechner consciously applied his psychological-spiritual paradigm to write about his own life. His three autobiographies, *The Sacred Journey* (1982), *Now and Then* (1983), and *Telling Secrets* (1991), trace with varying emphases the ways Buechner listens to his own life and what he hears there. The first two memoirs were written during his greatest crisis as an adult—the near fatal anorexia of his daughter—and although this is not specifically described until the third memoir, this experience accentuated his personal need to gain a deeper understanding of himself through psychotherapy and by writing his memoirs.

Buechner states that for him writing is a form of therapy. Through his writing he gets in touch with issues going on within him, and as he articulates these, he is able to see or hear them more clearly. At times, he assumes the role of the patient, exposing himself; at other times he is the therapist, setting up the psychotherapeutic interview, asking the questions, seeing connections between past and present. Because Buechner integrates psychotherapy with his belief in a personal, interactive God, it becomes a way for him to listen to his life, or in Allen's terminology, to reexperience his hurt trail to find his love story. As Buechner admitted in a 1989 interview, "A lot of what went into *The Sacred Journey* I went through first with a therapist. And then I shed tears about it, but they were as tears usually are, wonderfully healing" (Brown interview *Of Fiction and Faith* 51).

Although the first two autobiographies are chronologically organized in consecutive order, their focus is different. *Sacred Journey* traces his earliest childhood memories, his father's suicide when he was ten, the family's move to Bermuda, his years at Princeton and as a writer in New York, all connected by spiritual undercurrents leading up to his conversion. *Now and Then* explores his "vocation" and development as a writer with Christian concerns, specifically the lessons learned at Union Theological Seminary and Philips Exeter Academy, where his conscious theology came into being and found literary expression. In the third, psychologically oriented memoir *Telling Secrets,* Buechner describes the therapeutic/spiritual experience of writing the first two:

> It was at this time [during his daughter's illness] that I wrote two short autobiographical volumes called *The Sacred Journey* in 1982 and

> *Now and Then* in 1983, and they helped let a little light and air into the dark place where I was imprisoned. They gave me more of a sense than I had ever had before of how as far back as I could remember things had been stirring in my life that I was all but totally unaware of at the time. If anybody had predicted when I was an undergraduate at Princeton that I was going to be ordained as a minister ten years after graduation, I think I would have been flabbergasted. Yet as I wrote those two autobiographical volumes I found myself remembering small events as far back as early childhood which were even then leading me in something like that direction but so subtly and almost imperceptibly that it wasn't until decades had passed that I saw them for what they were . . . . The events were often so small that I was surprised to remember them, yet they turned out to have been road markers on a journey I didn't even know I was taking. The people involved in them were often people I had never thought of as having played particularly significant roles in my life yet looking back at them I saw that, for me, they had been life-givers, saints. (47-48)

According to Buechner, the therapeutic experience of writing the memoirs had much in common with psychotherapy, for in listening to one's life, one begins to "let a little light and air" into the past and consequently the present experience. The act of going back, of remembering, allowed Buechner to trace not only his hurt trail to face sad or difficult experiences, but also allowed him to begin to grasp his love story, the almost imperceptible but significant incidents of the spiritual stirrings in his life. Like the experience of psychotherapy as defined by Buechner and Allen, awareness of pain and sacredness (healing/meaning) went hand in hand.

According to Allen's psychological paradigm, humans are made in the image of God (*imago dei*) but because we live in a fallen world, the beginning point of therapy is awareness that life is wounded. Rather than denying pain, healing involves a conscious exploration of past hurts. For Buechner, the dominant wound of his childhood was his father's suicide, an experience so profound that he divides his life into "before" and "after" this event in his first memoir, *Sacred Journey*. The first section entitled "Once Below a Time," a phrase taken from Dylan Thomas's poem "Fern Hill," describes his experience as a child before his father's suicide as prelapsarian, an age of innocence: "Childhood's time is Adam and Eve's time before they left the garden for good and from that time on divided everything into before and after" (10). Here Buechner parallels psychological and theological realities.

Buechner expands the biblical analogy of Adam in Eden before the fall to describe his early childhood: "I had dominion then over all the earth and over every living thing that moves upon the earth" (11). The members of his immediate family "were the Atlases who held the world on their shoulders . . .the names they had were the names I gave them, I gave them also new selves to become—made my father a father, my mother a mother—and what they were apart from me, I no more knew or cared" (11). In Allen's paradigm, taken from Margaret Mahler's stages of object relations, this is the fusion stage, when the infant's identity stems completely from the caregiving parent. There has not yet been separation/individuation. For Buechner, this state is akin to the unbroken communion of innocence before the Fall, when Adam shares God's creative power through naming. In this context, Buechner includes his nanny, Mrs. Taylor, who taught him to "name the animals" and thus take dominion over them. As one of the first "saints" in his life, she sang him to sleep at night singing "'The Old Rugged Cross, ' which as far as I can remember was the only hymn I ever heard as the child of non-church-going parents, although I had no idea what a hymn was or what a cross was or why it was something to sing about in the dark" (13). On a literary level, during a year of illness, Buechner vividly entered an Edenic world through the Oz books by L. Frank Baum. The land of Oz, "where animals can speak, and magic is common as grass, and no one dies, was so much more real to me than the world of my own room" (14-15). There he grew to love his endearing hero, King Rinkitink, who became his prototypical hero in his own novels, triumphing over evil despite his foolishness and vulnerability. King Rinkitink and his friend Prince Inga of Pingaree possess three magic pearls: a blue one that conferred such strength that no power could resist it; a pink one that protected its owner from all dangers; and a pure white one that could speak words of great wisdom and helpfulness. "Never question the truth of what you fail to understand," the white pearl said when Rinkitink consulted it for the first time, "for the world is filled with wonders" (16). This theme comes up time and again in Buechner's writings. While the fantasy in the Oz books underscored the sense of mystery and wonder which is the privilege of childhood, they also provided links to a mature spiritual understanding. Buechner observes that the three pearls embodied the highest spiritual gifts described by Saint Paul in I Corinthians 13— faith, hope, and love (16).

Thus, in retrospect, even the Oz books expressed the spiritual (and psychological) truths he would later come to recognize in life itself, for he says:

> Nothing was more remote from my thought at this period than theological speculation...these books were all childhood or early boyhood reading, but certain patterns were set, certain rooms were made ready, so that when, years later, I came upon Saint Paul for the first time and heard him say, "God chose what is foolish in the world to shame the wise, God chose what is weak in the world to shame the strong, God chose what is low and despised in the world, even things that are not, to bring to nothing things that are," I had

the feeling that I knew something of what he was talking about. Something of the divine comedy that we are all of us involved in. Something of grace. (18)

The scriptural pattern of God choosing vulnerable/wounded persons also reflects Buechner's understanding of psychotherapy: it is only when you admit you need help that you can receive it. According to his childhood experience, even in the time of innocence, this message of wisdom/ vulnerability was being received through literature.

The second section of *The Sacred Journey* entitled "Once Upon a Time" deals with the suicide of his father in 1936 when Buechner was ten. This was the cataclysmic event which brought the end of innocence and the beginning of time, "the first tick of the clock that measures everything into before and after, and at that exact moment my once-below a time ended and my once-upon-a-time began" (39). Reflecting on the experience of his father's death in poetic prose which combines his psychological and spiritual understanding, Buechner states,

> God speaks to us through our lives, we often too easily say. Something speaks anyway, spells out some sort of godly or godforsaken meaning to us through the alphabet of our years, but often it takes many years and many further spellings out before we start to glimpse, or think we do, a little of what that meaning is. Even then we glimpse it only dimly, like the first trace of dawn on the rim of night, or even then it is a meaning that we cannot fix and be sure of once and for all because it is always incarnate meaning and thus as alive and changing as we are ourselves alive and changing .
> . . .
> When somebody you love dies, Mark Twain

said, it is like when your house burns down; it isn't for years that you realize the full extent of your loss. For me it was longer than for most, if indeed I have realized it fully even yet, and in the meanwhile the loss came to get buried so deep in me that after a time I scarcely ever took it out to look at it at all, let alone to speak of it. . . .

And then by grace or by luck or by some cool, child's skill for withdrawing from anything too sharp or puzzling to deal with, I stopped remembering. (41)

Here Buechner is describing his experience of burying pain, his hurt self, in order to survive. However, a positive defense in childhood can later become counterproductive to mature growth, which is why Buechner needed to feel the full extent of the loss as an adult, an experience he describes in *Telling Secrets*. In *Sacred Journey*, however, the emphasis is on the positive ways God's grace was working in his life, despite the sad experiences, and for the child this meant covering pain until an appropriate time to uncover and cope with it as an adult. Thus in this chronological memoir, Buechner follows the graphic portrayal of his father's death with an equally graphic description of his experience of grace: the magic land of Bermuda in the 1930s, which for Buechner was a land of Oz, a balm of Gilead, a foretaste of Paradise on earth:

Out of my father's death there came, for me, a new and, in many ways, a happier life. The shock of his death faded and so did those feelings about it. . . . I cannot say the grief faded because, in a sense, I had not yet, unlike my brother, really felt that grief. That was not to happen for thirty years or more. But the grief was postponed, allowed to sink beneath the whole bright accumulation of the Bermuda years . . . . This is the reality of those

> years as I look back at them, and part of their reality for me is that all the healing and strengthening that came my way then came my way largely as a gift and as a gift that implies a giver. (53-54)

Here Buechner is describing the psychological dynamics of his early experience in light of his Christian faith. It is his articulation of the dynamics of the past, not the experiences per se, that provides the unique insights that are later revealed in his novels. These novels are far more than a transparent psychological replay of his life, which would not produce fiction of outstanding quality. Similarly in his memoir, he describes the Bermuda experience in spiritual terms—grace, gift, paradise. Although he also articulates the "psychological ways" (i.e., Freudian) to look at this experience, his rhetorical nod, "you could say," indicates a purely psychological perspective does not fully explain what happened:

> You could say that the trauma of the father's suicide was such that the boy, unable to come to terms with his own feelings, repressed them to the extent that they were bound to cause psychological problems later on. You could speak in terms of Oedipal conflict and say that part of the reason the boy seemed to recover from his grief as quickly as he did was that, with his father's death, he got what, subconsciously, he had of course always wanted, which was his mother to himself. And you could say that one consequence of that might well have been just such a residue of anxiety and guilt as might in later years lead him to seek consolation in religious fantasy, to dream up for himself a father in Heaven to replace the one he had lost. (55)

For Buechner, by acknowledging a psychoanalytic interpretation, he diffuses it and allows the experience to be interpreted in a larger spiritual context. Here his subtle prose style, the skillful use of understatement, sets him apart from the Freudian literary critics or others who have viewed literature and life within a purely psychoanalytic paradigm. Ever a literary artist, Buechner's contribution is his unique way of expressing a psychological perspective, which instead of discrediting biblical principles, complements them.

> Which of us can look at our own religion or lack of it without seeing in it the elements of wish fulfillment? Which of us can look back at our own lives without seeing in them the role of blind chance and dumb luck? But faith, says the author of the Epistle to the Hebrews, is "the assurance of things hoped for, the conviction of things not seen," and looking back at those distant years I choose not to deny, either, the compelling sense of an unseen giver and a series of hidden gifts as not only part of their reality, but the deepest part of all. (56)

In part three of *Sacred Journey* entitled "Beyond Time," Buechner summarizes his emerging theme, echoing the words of Shakespeare's Caliban in the *Tempest* and Jesus in the scriptures:

> What each of them [events of our lives] might be thought to mean separately is less important than what they all mean together. At the very least they mean this: mean *listen*. Listen. Your life is happening. . . . A journey, years long, has brought each of you through thick and thin to this moment in time as mine has also brought me. Think back on that journey. Listen back to the sounds and sweet airs of your journey that give delight and

hurt not and to those too that give no delight at all and hurt like Hell. *Be not affeard.* The music of your life is subtle and elusive and like no other—not a song with words but a song without words, a singing, clattering music to gladden the heart or turn the heart to stone, to haunt you perhaps with echoes of a vaster, farther music of which it is part.

The question is not whether the things that happen to you are chance things or God's things because, of course, they are both at once. There is no chance thing through which God cannot speak—even the walk from the house to the garage that you have walked ten thousand times before, even the moments when you cannot believe there is a God who speaks at all anywhere. He speaks, I believe, and the words he speaks are incarnate in the flesh and blood of our selves and of our own footsore and sacred journeys. We cannot live our lives constantly looking back, listening back, lest we be turned to pillars of longing and regret, but to live without listening at all is to live deaf to the fullness of the music. Sometimes we avoid listening for fear of what we may hear; sometimes for fear that we may hear nothing at all but the empty rattle of our own feet on the pavement. But be not affeard says Caliban, nor is he the only one to say it. "Be not afraid," says another, "for lo, I am with you always, even unto the end of the world." He says he is with us on our journeys. He says he has been with us since each of our journeys began. Listen for him. Listen to the sweet and bitter airs of your present and your past for the sound of him. (77-78)

Interwoven into the Buechnerian style is the natural integration not only of Scripture, but also quotes from Shakespeare. Words of Caliban from *The Tempest* as above, or King Lear on his moment of insight during the storm, or Graham Greene's whiskey priest, exemplify Buechner's technique of showing literature as a way to get at essentials. This appreciation of literature as a vehicle for listening to life parallels his view of psychotherapy and spirituality—all increase our perception of the themes, even the truths, being played out in our experience.

At Princeton, Buechner majored in English. Doodles in his class notes reveal traces of the themes that would later be expressed in his writings (see frontispiece).[1] Even then Buechner was fascinated with images of Eden and Christianity. Jacob's stone stair may be symbolically present, as is a possible self-portrait under the words "cerebral Kortex" [sic]. The following page in the notebook reveals an early alphabet of grace: floating titles and authors' names, random literary expressions from his college studies are juxtaposed with lines of the alphabet in different scripts and the faces of characters. The subconscious musings of the artist, visually expressed, later find expression in his writings.

The last section of *The Sacred Journey* relates Buechner's experience at Princeton, which was interrupted by a short stint in the army during World War II. The main focus of the section is on his growing awareness of God. Buechner explains:

> Beyond time is the phrase that I have used to describe this leg of my journey because it was then that I think I first began to have a pale version of the experience that Saint Paul describes in his letter to the Philippians. "Work out your own salvation with fear and trembling ... for God is at work in you both to will and to work for his good pleasure." (94-95)

Buechner's awareness that a power beyond time was working

"to achieve its own aim through my aimless life" came into focus as he began to write his first novel and the sense of plot developed "and, beyond that, a sense that perhaps life itself has a plot—that events of our lives, random and witless as they generally seem, have a shape and direction of their own, are seeking to show us something, lead us somewhere" (95).

In later writings, Buechner has stated memory is the key component needed to effectively listen to one's life, whether in psychotherapy, which deals with the recovery and healing of painful repressed memories, or in spiritual awareness of the ways God has been present in and through past experiences. In his last memoir, his third remembering, he cites again the importance of memory, for it allows us to both bless and be blessed by the past, and is not only "therapeutic but sacred" (TS 34).

Buechner's sacred journey culminates as he hears a sermon one Sunday morning. Looking back, he remembers the minister said Jesus Christ refused the crown that Satan offered him in the wilderness, but he is king nonetheless because again and again he is crowned in the hearts of the people who believe in him. And that inward coronation takes place "among confession, and tears, and great laughter." Buechner states that he suddenly found that a door had been open all along which he had only just then stumbled upon:

> What I found was what I had already half seen or less than half, in many places over my twenty-seven years without ever clearly knowing what it was that I was seeing... Something in me recoils from using such language, but here at the end I am left with no other way of saying it than that what I found finally was Christ. Or was found. It hardly seems to matter which. There are other words for describing what happened to me— psychological words, historical words, poetic words, but in honesty as well as in faith I am

reduced to the word that is his name because no other seems to account for the experience so fully. (110-111)

Here Buechner seems to be diminishing the psychotherapeutic analysis in favor of straightforward Christian terminology, and this is the position he ultimately takes. Just as memory is "not just therapeutic but sacred," the final reality for Buechner is spiritual, although he uses the psychological to engage, explicate, and clarify the spiritual.

Following his conversion experience, Buechner enrolled in Union Theological Seminary in New York City, and the subsequent stages of his journey are the subject of his second memoir, *Now and Then*. Buechner's growing faith, expressed through his seminary studies, work with the poor in East Harlem, and finally as the chaplain and director of the department of religion at Phillips Exeter Academy provide the basic events. The title *Now and Then* comes from Buechner's professor at Union, the theologian Paul Tillich "to the effect that here and there even in our world, and now and then even in ourselves, we catch glimpses of a New Creation, which, fleeting as those glimpses are apt to be, give us hope both for this life and for whatever life may await us later on" (NT 109).

The second memoir *Now and Then* more overtly traces the development of Buechner's theology, the experience of the New Creation, which came to be expressed increasingly in his writings. In this memoir of his vocation, Buechner describes the ways his early novels came into being and the themes, gleaned from his own life, which he wove into them. Like the first memoir, listening to one's life for themes, patterns and signals of spiritual direction is central, but this time it is more conscious and focused on its expression within the context of his novels, not just his life, that Buechner feels the voice speaking. He explains the process of creating fiction:

... novels, for me, start—as Robert Frost said his poems did—with a lump in the throat. I don't start with some theological axe to grind, but with a deep, wordless feeling for some aspect of my own experience that has moved me. Then, out of the shadows, a handful of characters starts to emerge, then various possible relationships between them, then a setting maybe, and lastly, out of those relationships, the semblance at least of a plot. Like any other serious novelist, I try to be as true as I can to life as I have known it. I write not as a propagandist but as an artist.

On the other hand—and here is where I feel I must be so careful—since my ordination, I have written consciously as a Christian, as an evangelist, or apologist, even. That does not mean that I preach in my novels, which would make for neither good novels nor good preaching. On the contrary, I lean over backwards not to. I choose as my characters (or out of my dreams do they choose me?) men and women whose feet are as much of clay as mine are because they are the only people I can begin to understand. As a novelist no less than as a teacher, I try not to stack the deck unduly but always let doubt and darkness have their say along with faith and hope, not just because it is good apologetics—woe to him who tries to make it look simple and easy—but because to do it any other way would be to be less than true to the elements of doubt and darkness that exist in myself no less than in others. (*Now and Then* 59-60)

Buechner's third memoir goes beneath the external happenings of his life to take a deeper psychological look at unconscious conflicts and issues which acted out in maladaptive ways. Like Allen's concept of the need to break the false self, which was created as a defense against the real, hurt self, Buechner seeks to peel back the daily reality of his life, to see the powerful dynamics being played out beneath the surface. His third memoir *Telling Secrets* (1991) deals with the psychological workings of events in the first two and his subsequent experiences. Again, Buechner is interested in tracing the "plot" of his life, this time with an emphasis on the underlying psychological explanations which tie the chronological narrative together like the plot of a novel. Here Buechner seeks to dig beneath the surface, to ferret out the secrets, which one keeps from the world and from oneself. He is seeking to look beneath the "highly edited version which we put forth in hope that the world will find it more acceptable than the real thing" (TS 2) to reveal "the secret of who we truly and fully are and little by little come to accept" (3).

Beginning again with the key event of his childhood, his father's suicide, this time Buechner looks at the ways he and his family reacted to it, which as a child he seemed quickly to forget. However, with psychological eyeglasses, Buechner observes: "Because none of the three of us ever talked about how we had felt about him when he was alive or how we felt about him now that he wasn't, those feelings soon disappeared too and went underground along with the memories" (9). Buechner describes repression, a defense against pain, and makes a diagnosis of a dysfunctional family in terms of rules borrowed from the recovery movement: "Don't talk, don't trust, don't feel is supposed to be the unwritten law of families that for one reason or another have gone out of whack, and certainly it was our law" (9).

These "laws" often characterize a dysfunctional family system, described by Alcoholics Anonymous (therapy program for alcoholics and other substance abusers) and Al Anon (therapy program for the spouses and adult children of alcoholics) which highlight the maladaptive ways codependent families seek to cover up a family secret (usually the presence of an addicted member).

As the child of an alcoholic father, and father of very ill daughter, Buechner later found support and strength from the recovery movement. Citing its relevance, he observes:

> "adult children" is an odd phrase meaning adults who still carry with them many of the confusions and fears and hurts of their childhood, and one of the luckiest things I ever did, to use one kind of language—one of God's most precious gifts to me, to use another—was to discover that I was one of them and that there were countless others like me who were there when I needed them and by whom I also was needed. I have found more spiritual nourishment and strength and understanding among them than I have found anywhere else for a long time. (94-95)

Prior to his involvement in psychotherapy or the recovery movement, however, Buechner may have unconsciously sought to begin his own healing (although he would not have recognized this at the time), by sharing the family secret of his father's suicide in one of his novels. His mother's response and his subsequent guilt were characteristic of the dysfunctional family:

> Don't talk, trust, feel was the law we lived by, and woe to the one who broke it. Twenty-two years later in a novel called *The Return of Ansel Gibbs* I told a very brief and fictionalized version of my father's death and the most accurate words I can find to describe my mother's reaction to it is fury. For days she could hardly bring herself to speak to me, and when she did, it was with words of great bitterness. As she saw it, I had betrayed a sacred trust, and though I might have defended myself by saying that the story was after

> all as much mine as his son to tell as it was hers as his widow to keep hidden, I not only didn't say any such things but never even considered such things. I felt as much of a traitor as she charged me with being and at the age of thirty-two was as horrified at what I had done as if I had been a child of ten. I was full of guilt and remorse and sure that in who-knows-what grim and lasting way I would be made to suffer for what I had done. (10)

Referring to his mother's psychological refusal to see or hear painful realities, Buechner describes how as a woman in her eighties, his mother refused to wear her hearing aids and would actually close her eyes when talking to him. His mother's overt forms of denial provide a psychological and literary transition into his own denial during the painful experience of his daughter's anorexia nervosa:

> In the mid 1970s, as a father of three teenage children and a husband of some twenty years standing by then, I would have said that my hearing was pretty good, that I could hear not only what my wife and children were saying but lots of things they weren't saying too. I would have said that I saw fairly well what was going on inside our house and what was going on inside me.... But in certain other ways, I came to learn, I was as deaf as my mother was with her little gold purse full of hearing aids none of which really ever worked very well, and though I did not shut my eyes when I talked to people the way she did, I shut them without knowing it to a whole dimension of the life that my wife and I and our children were living together on a green hillside in Vermont during those years. (19)

Buechner calls the events going on during this time a "fearsome blessing" because during his daughter's illness, he was forced to see and hear what had previously been too painful. One blessing was the therapeutic experience of writing the novel *Godric*:

> Nothing I've ever written came out of a darker time or brought me more light and comfort. It also—far more than I realized at the time I wrote it—brought me a sharper glimpse than I had ever had before of the crucial role my father has always played in my life and continues to play in my life. ...[In writing passages about Godric's losing his father] I was writing more than I had known I knew with the result that the book was not only a word from me—my words painstakingly chosen and arranged into sentences by me alone—but also a word out of such a deep and secret part of who I am that It seemed also a world to me.... A book you write out of the depths of who you are, like a dream you dream out of those same depths, is entirely your own creation.... But it seems to me nonetheless that a book you write, like a dream you dream, can have more healing and truth and wisdom in it at least for yourself than you feel in any way responsible for.
>
> A large part of the truth that *Godric* had for me was the truth that although death ended my father, it has never ended my relationship with my father—a secret I had never so clearly understood before. (21-22)

Identifying with Frank Baum's Cowardly Lion, bound with ropes and plagued by the tormenting monkeys, Buechner faces the painful experience of watching his daughter waste away, "a victim of Buchenwald:"

> ... the Cowardly Lion got more and more afraid and sad, felt more and more helpless. No rational argument, no dire medical warning, no pleading or cajolery or bribery would make this young woman he loved eat normally again but only seemed to strengthen her determination not to, this young woman on whose life his own in so many ways depended. He could not solve her problem because he was of course himself part of her problem. . . . Then finally, when she had to be hospitalized, a doctor called one morning to say that unless they started feeding her against her will, she would die. It was as clear-cut as that. Tears ran down the Cowardly Lion's face as he stood with the telephone at his ear. His paws were tied. The bat-winged monkeys hovered. (24)
>
> My anorectic daughter was in danger of starving to death, and without knowing it, so was I. I wasn't living my own life any more because I was so caught up in hers. If in refusing to eat she was mad as a hatter, I was if anything madder still because whereas in some sense she knew what she was doing to herself, I knew nothing at all about what I was doing to myself. She had given up food. I had virtually given up doing anything in the way of feeding myself humanly. (25)

Being forced out of the defenses and denial, Buechner comes to face his codependency, the secret bondage inherited from his dysfunctional family. Psychologically, this difficult experience tore down the last remnants of his false self, to leave his hurt wounded self exposed. What could be more devastating than for him to watch helplessly as his daughter slowly committed suicide, an agonizing reenactment of the most traumatic loss of his childhood?

Near the end of *Telling Secrets* Buechner describes the specific techniques of psychotherapy which helped him to reconnect with the past and thus listen to his life on a deeper level:

> A lot of what [my therapist] did was not just to help me remember forgotten parts of my childhood and to recapture some of the feelings connected with them, which I had discovered as a child that I would do well to forget, but also to suggest certain techniques for accomplishing that. One such technique that worked especially well for me was writing about those distant days with my left hand. My right hand is my grown-up hand—a writer's hand, a minister's hand—but when I wrote with the left hand, I found that what tended to come out was as artless and basic as the awkward scrawl it came out in. It was as if some of my secrets had at last found a way of communicating with me directly. She suggested on one occasion that when I got home I should try writing out a dialogue with my father, using my left hand for both of our parts . . . . (98)

Use of the left hand to reenact feelings of childhood vulnerability, writing letters or dialogues to or with someone from the past, is a frequently used therapeutic technique. It is often used as part of the grieving process, when the therapist believes the patient has an aborted grief reaction, and needs to do the grief work necessary for healing. In studying dying patients, Kubler-Ross researched the stages of grief they go through when confronted by their own death: denial, anger, bargaining, and acceptance. Buechner's aborted grief reaction, experienced in relation to his father's death, was accentuated by the repetition of psychological dynamics and fear of loss associated with the illness of his daughter. The dialogue exercise, written with the left hand, allowed Buechner to reconnect with his father, and then to say goodbye.

A vivid dream allowed Buechner the opportunity to have a similar experience in separating, saying goodbye, to his mother. In both experiences, he was left with a deeper feeling of peace—there was no need to worry. To use Allen's paradigm, Buechner was moving from the House of Fear to the House of Love.

In addition to the healing he experienced in professional psychotherapy which taught him the value of memory through several spiritual experiences, Buechner learned to trust God, to have faith when all seemed darkest. Secondly, he learned that unlike his love, or lovesickness, the "realistic, tough, conscientious" love the doctors and nurses exhibited in treating his daughter was closer to what Jesus meant by love than was his own.

Thus Buechner's view of psychotherapy based on his own experience has a spiritual source: it is one way God heals memory and the past:

> ... I am inclined to believe that God's chief purpose in giving us memory is to enable us to go back in time so that if we didn't play those roles right the first time round, we can still have another go at it now. We cannot undo our old mistakes or their consequences any more than we can erase old wounds that we have both suffered and inflicted, but through the power that memory gives us of thinking, feeling, imagining our way back through time we can at long last finally finish with the past in the sense of removing its power to hurt us and other people and to stunt our growth as human beings.
>
> The sad things that happened long ago will always remain part of who we are just as the glad and gracious things will too, but instead of being a burden of guilt, recrimination, and regret that

make us constantly stumble as we go, even the saddest things can become, once we have made peace with them, a source of wisdom and strength for the journey that still lies ahead. It is through memory that we are able to reclaim much of our lives that we have long since written off by finding that in everything that has happened to us over the years God was offering us possibilities of new life and healing which, though we may have missed them at the time, we can still choose and be brought to life by and healed by all these

Another way of saying it, perhaps, is that memory makes it possible for us both to bless the past, even those parts of it that we have always felt cursed by, and also to be blessed by it. If this kind of remembering sounds like what psychotherapy is all about, it is because of course it is, but I think it is also what the forgiveness of sins is all about—the interplay of God's forgiveness of us and our forgiveness of God and each other. To see how God's mercy was for me buried deep even in my father's death was not just to be able to forgive my father for dying and God for letting him die so young and without hope and all the people like my mother who were involved in his death but also to be able to forgive myself for all the years I had failed to air my crippling secret so that then, however slowly and uncertainly, I could start to find healing. It is in the experience of such healing that I believe we experience also God's loving forgiveness of us, and insofar as memory is the doorway to both experiences, it becomes not just therapeutic but sacred. (32-34)

Although an important part of learning to listen to one's life, psychotherapy is ultimately subordinate to spirituality. Thus "not just therapeutic but sacred" is what for Buechner is the power of memory, as it is used in psychotherapy or spirituality. In both, memory is used to expose the real hurt self to feel the suffering of the past, for as Allen has found, in therapy one must work one's hurt trail before one can discover one's love story (the healing of memories and forgiveness through the love of God). It is the central paradox of Christianity: unless a grain of wheat falls into the ground and dies, it abides alone. But if it dies, it bears much fruit—the paradox of death and resurrection, the paradox of memory.

Finally, beyond remembering and reclaiming the past, listening to one's life involves the ability to find the still place within, the holy place in us which retains a reflection of the *imago dei*. Buechner cites the things that can get us in tune, making us aware of the presence of God: a work of art, beauty, sometimes sorrow or joy, sometimes just the quiet quality of a moment, the quiet of trust and peace.

Buechner's psychological and spiritual perspective sheds light on the way he intuitively writes his fiction. To reduce his novels to mere manifestations of his psyche fails to do them justice, however. As literature, the novels are more than fictionalized memoirs or Christian parables. They are significant literary creations with merit in and of themselves.

3

The Early Novels: Where Dreams Come From

> ... Tristram Bone, the hero of that earliest novel, appears on the first page seated in a barber chair facing the mirror in a white sheet that hangs from his shoulders like a robe. "The mirror reflected what seemed at first a priest," is the way the book begins, and insofar as what the mirror also reflected was an image, albeit an unconscious one, of myself, I cannot help thinking of that opening sentence as itself just such a whisper, as the first faint intimation from God knows where of the direction my life was even then starting to take me, although if anyone had said so at the time, I would have thought he was mad. (SJ 96)

Buechner's novels written between 1950 and 1970 prefigure his psychological and spiritual themes. In these early novels, a third-person omniscient narrator reveals how the characters seek to listen to their past and present experiences. Through self-examination and introspection they listen to themselves in a haphazard way, without the psychological or spiritual understanding of the protagonists in the later novels, but their impulse to listen to their lives to discern meaning is the same. Following these early novels, Buechner's autobiographical journal *Alphabet of Grace,* his subsequent novel *Lion Country,* and his experience of psychotherapy mark a turning point affecting his future approach to writing and to listening to his life.[1]

This profound change in Buechner's later writing can be appreciated when contrasted with his earlier novels. Although all five early novels foreshadow Buechner's concept listening to one's life through psychological and spiritual awareness, this is most clearly prefigured in *A Long Day's Dying*, *The Return of Ansel Gibbs*, and *The Final Beast*.

Even in his earliest novel, *A Long Day's Dying* (1950), Tristram Bone, the protagonist, is listening to his life. He notes vague glimmers of something spiritual as a reflected image of himself. Buechner uses psychological aspects of character (Bone's pervasive introspection) to reveal spiritual receptivity which he later came to see subconsciously also represented his own spiritual yearnings. In terms of Buechner's use of psychological spirituality, Bone's introspective thought life leans in a psychological direction as he ponders issues of the past, dilemmas of the present, and worries about the future. He is an alienated modern man, attempting to listen to his life.

All five novels written prior to *Alphabet of Grace* (1970) are told from the perspective of a third-person omniscient narrator structured to reveal the major characters' thoughts. Separate sections or chapters focus on the mental musings of a particular character. *A Long Day's Dying* begins with Tristram Bone's thoughts about himself as he gazes at the mirror in the barber's chair. Draped with the salon robe, he is described as having the appearance of a priest. We are told this by the narrator, and Tristram himself notices this, setting the metaphorical stage for the protagonist's subconscious leanings in a spiritual direction. Later we are presented with Maroo's inner world, her desire to foster her grandson and her wariness of the influence of his cynical young

The Early Novels: Where Dreams Come From

professor. Through her thoughts and the narratorial comment, readers are presented with the insights of a "wise soul," the anchor of the family, as she listens to her life. We also move into the world of Steitler, the young professor, to learn his perspective and thoughts. Actual conversations between characters cover more than they reveal, but mental solliloquies allow readers to hear their thoughts. Conscious and unconscious workings of the various characters' minds reveal alienation and lack of communication as a central theme in this first novel.

Buechner's third novel, *The Return of Ansel Gibbs* (1958), is also told in the third person, but ambivalence rather than alienation is the protagonist's tragic flaw. Gibbs, the President's Cabinet nominee, speaks to journalists, adding they are not to quote him. The omniscient narrator comments, " and thus he both said and in effect unsaid what they had come to hear. This was his way, some might have held: rarely seeming to follow any single course, but whenever possible, replacing a plus with a plus-or-minus, making of that little mathematical cross of Lorraine a kind of heraldic emblem" (3). The narrator here underscores Gibbs' ambivalence. Then we are privy to the thoughts of Porter Hoye, Gibbs' legal advisor, who values facts, not vagaries of spirituality or emotion. In chapter two the narrator reviews the past history and inner life of Gibbs' daughter Anne and her romantic interest in Robin Tripp. In time we hear the righteous thoughts of Gibbs' old religious professor and mentor Kuykendall, then the mixed motives and insecurities of Hoye at the hotel bath. Piece by piece, the mental lives and motivations of the main characters are revealed, as one by one the reader hears their thoughts and the narratorial assessment. We never hear the inner thoughts of Robin Tripp, the mystery character who instigates much of the plot, but we discover his issues through his heart-to-heart talk with Anne. As Robin Tripp peels open the issues of his chameleon self, the lasting effect of his father's suicide reflects what Buechner will write about his own experience in his memoirs several years later.

In this sense these early novels are psychological—even

"densely" psychological—as the inner monologues and dialogues between characters deal extensively with their thoughts about the past, their ambivalence about the present, and their fears about the future. Although they arrive at various insights, there is no reference to professional psychotherapy or wisdom about grief and suffering as is present in Buechner's later novels. Characters trapped by their pasts or by ineffective communication gain understanding as they think deeply about their lives. In *The Return of Ansel Gibbs*, Robin reveals the traumas of his early childhood and father's suicide to Anne and thus begins to put away his protective and multi-faceted false selves. Gibbs' introspective dialogues show the painful process of coming to face himself and then the forthright input from friends (his community) brings him to self-acceptance and finally action.

In words paralleling Allen's concept of facing the wounded self, 1958 reviewer A. C. Spectorsky noted that the major characters in *The Return of Ansel Gibbs* are "beset by the crucial need to discover—and to face—the real, the inner self. Each, in his way, achieves that goal" (21). As a novelist, Buechner was grappling with psychological issues in his characters, but he had not yet been in therapy nor had he developed the necessary writing techniques to create the psychological-spiritual impact of his later novels.

Nevertheless, in terms of Buechner's own development as a person, psychological and spiritual forces can be seen interacting even when he wrote A *Long Day's Dying*, his first and most commercially successful novel. In terms of the outworkings of his unconscious, he recalls:

> .... it was in no overt way autobiographical. Instead, like all the novels I have written since, it came from the same part of myself that dreams come from and by a process scarcely less obscure. I labor very hard at the actual writing of them, but

The Early Novels: Where Dreams Come From

> the plot and characters and general feeling of them come from somewhere deeper down and farther away than conscious effort. (SJ 98)

Buechner's deft intuitive handling of the psychological emptiness of the modern world found appreciative response in the popular and literary press. Published in January, 1950, by Alfred Knopf when Buechner was only 23, the novel was an immediate critical and commercial success, hailed a masterpiece of literary modernism. Rave reviews compared its young author to Henry James and Marcel Proust. By February it was on the *New York Times* list of best sellers. Buechner's photograph appeared in *Life*, *Time*, *Newsweek*, and major newspapers across the United States, giving him recognition as the most promising young American writer of his generation. For example, writing a glowing review for *The New York Times Book Review* (Jan. 8, 1950), David Daiches, an authority on the history of English literature, wrote:

> This first novel by a young man of 23 is a remarkable piece of work. There is a quality of civilized perception here, a sensitive and plastic handling of English prose and an ability to penetrate to the evanescent core of a human situation, all proclaiming major talent.... The author's main objective seems to be to explore the implications of sensibilities which operate without a clearly perceived moral base. This is, of course, one of the central themes of modern fiction.... all in all this is a work of real art, fine sensitivity and uncanny human understanding. Mr. Buechner is more than the " promising young novelist" reviewers like to hail. He has already arrived and this reviewer at least is going to take the enormous risk of making the pronouncement that with *A*

Long Day's Dying Frederick Buechner has established himself as a major literary figure.

As critics like Daiches were quick to point out, *A Long Day's Dying* had a highly developed literary quality. Trained in the study of literature at Lawrenceville and Princeton where he was an English major, Buechner was well schooled in literary craft. His love for seventeenth-century English poetry and prose and knowledge of late nineteenth- and early twentieth-century writers shaped his literary sensibility, as noted in his Jamesian style and polished prose. Nurtured on New Critical sensibilities (R. P. Blackmur was one of his professors), Buechner valued organic unity, reflected in theme, imagery, and plot structure, and his appreciation of paradox and ambiguity found fertile expression in this story of upper-class emptiness in an Ivy League Eden. As a young modernist writing at mid-century, Buechner's themes of alienation and social hollowness reflected his own experience and his reading of poets such as T.S. Eliot. At the same time, he articulates the "operation of sensibilities which operate without a clearly perceived moral base" with a sense of sadness and loss not found in many other modernist writers.

Yet in this novel, religious imagery is ubiquitous, intentionally and ironically promising more than it can deliver. Not only is the protagonist Tristram Bone metaphorically introduced as a priest, but significant interaction between characters occurs during visits to the Cloisters, a medieval art museum in New York City. Although not a comic novel, Buechner's humor is subtly evident, as Tristram Bone awkwardly gets his hand stuck while touching the hand of a large wooden sculpture of a saint. Trying to untangle himself, he falls to his knee and silently utters a semi-prayer, which the Judas figure George Motley watches from his hiding place and mockingly reveals to Elizabeth Poor, the beautiful woman both men seek to impress. As a malevolent court jester, he later tells Bone of Elizabeth's sexual impropriety with a young professor, a betrayal that destroys all hopes for trusting relationships.

Like all Buechner's future protagonists, Tristram Bone is a

"spiritual" hero, who is sensitive, compassionate, and in his own way, noble. According to Buechner, he was

> the lineal descendant... of King Rinkitink [of Oz] and the Emperor Claudius and Louis the Sixteenth... who I have come more and more to believe... was a kind of image not of myself as I was but of myself as with some part of me I dreamed of being. I was on the thin side, actually, and in countless ways vulnerable, but he was fat, and his fatness seemed armor somehow against the perils of the world without and at the same time a powerful insulation against the fires that rage in the world within. (SJ 94)

Bone's size metaphorically represents a kind of protection and insulation against conflicts from within and without. Buechner has not yet been in therapy and as a young man he assumes the best way to deal with emotional pain is to insulate oneself against it.[2] Ironically this jovial fat man's name is Tristram Bone. "Tristram" for "sorrowful" (Latin, *tristis*), and Bone signifying malnourishment and his less than fulfilling human relationships. In fact his main companion is his pet monkey, Simon, whom he dresses in a dinner jacket to entertain the guests at his party. Ironically, after the guests leave, the monkey commits suicide by imitating the mock suicidal gesture of his master. Bereft of his closest companion (and alter ego), Bone goes to Maroo on her sickbed for advice on how to live after this loss, but she dies without understanding his quest. Suicide plays a poignant role in this and almost all of Buechner's subsequent books. Psychological issues in Buechner's life are beginning to be revealed in his fiction, but the spiritual aspects of listening to one's life are embryonic. Even so, Buechner's use of spiritual and psychological themes are germane to his purpose in writing *A Long Day's Dying,* for they offer a diagnosis of the spiritual hunger and lost condition of modern humanity.

Although his characters are trying to listen to their lives to find purpose and meaning, they only hear themselves and their own thoughts. Tristram's thoughts portray his desire for kindness and goodness, but there is no evidence of God's intervention or answer to his rote prayers. He personifies literary modernism's empty and ineffective spirituality. For example, Bone is celibate and superficially resembles a priest. When Elizabeth looks at him later on "a priest he seemed for a moment, or a saint," (49) but the only fat saint she can think of is Aquinas. Later in his immense red dressing robe, he has the appearance of a Roman Catholic cardinal. He arranges a meeting with Stelizer at the Cloisters near the unicorn tapestries (symbol of Christ) where he queries the young professor like a priest hearing confession. Thinking Stelizer is homosexually involved with Leander, Elizabeth's son, Bone talks about sin, protecting the innocent, and the possibility of endangering souls. Like St. Francis, Bone communes with birds and is a patron of an aviary. Also because the plot is a play on the Philomela myth[3], birds are present to represent transformation, especially as Maroo dies.

Yet these religious sensibilities lack a moral base, as Daiches observed. Myers comments: "Tristram Bone is presented as a priest-like symbol, but he saves no one, least of all himself" (13). Elizabeth briefly considers confessing to Bone, hoping to find forgiveness and love, but then decides against it. In creating Bone as an ineffectual priest, who talks elaborately but cannot act, who foolishly bows to a wooden saint which he secretly wants to kick and deface, Buechner is commenting on the bankruptcy of modern spirituality. According to Ihab Hassan, "This is the existential form of a quest suspended in a vacuum more terrifying than interstellar spaces. For all its baroque richness, *A Long Day's Dying* is a novel about the experience of nothingness" (161). Whereas John Aldrich criticizes Buechner's characterization of Bone for being ineffectual and a failure, that is exactly Buechner's point. Like Graham Greene's whiskey priest, all Buechner's saints have feet of clay. In Bone's case, however, the power and the glory are not yet manifested.

The Early Novels: Where Dreams Come From

As Myers and others have noted, Buechner's ongoing theme of sanctifying the profane means the "religious dimension of his work is present from the beginning, even in writing produced before he had formally studied religion" (8). Yet as Hassan points out, Christian beliefs are implied rather than articulated, represented by ecclesiastical symbols and yearnings for decency rather than life changing experience. (154).

In this novel, the hero is a sensitive idealist, whose inability to act or articulate his desires results in ineffectual relationships. Although most critics saw Tristram Bone as a pathetic figure, Buechner has maintained the protagonist was noble and sympathetic. Doodles of his personage, which appear in Buechner's Princeton class notes and the handwritten manuscript bear a dignified appearance and it is interesting to note that in two separate places Buechner states that Bone represented a part of himself and his own subconscious spiritual yearnings.

The interaction of its spiritual and psychological themes is reflected in the title *A Long Day's Dying,* taken from the most famous religious poem in the English language, Milton's *Paradise Lost*. Adam's speech, which Buechner used as the epigraph for the novel, indicates the tragic implications facing Adam and Eve after the Fall, as they face a "slow-pac'd evil, a long day's dying to augment our pain." Adam tells Eve:

> But rise, let us no more contend, nor blame
> Each other, blamed enough elsewhere, but strive
> In offices of love how we may lighten
> Each other's burden in our share of woe:
> Since this day's death denounc'd, if aught I see,
> Will prove no sudden, but a slow-pac'd evil,
> A long day's dying to augment our pain,
> And to our seed, (O hapless seed!), deriv'd.
> *Paradise Lost* (Book X, line 958ff)

Writing thirty years later in his memoir *Sacred Journey*, Buechner explains why he chose this title in terms of the psychological interaction of his novel's alienated characters:

> I took the title from a passage in *Paradise Lost* where Adam says to Eve that their expulsion from Paradise "will prove no sudden but a slow pac'd evil,/ A long day's dying to augment our pain," and with the exception of the old lady Maroo, what all the characters seem to be dying of is loneliness, emptiness, sterility, and such preoccupation with themselves and their own problems that they are unable to communicate with each other about anything that really matters to them very much. I am sure that I chose such a melancholy theme partly because it seemed effective and fashionable, but I have no doubt that, like dreams generally, it also reflected the way I felt about at least some dimension of my own life and the lives of those around me. (SJ 98)

Some of the religious imagery and concern with spiritual issues as well as the novel's baroque style reflects Buechner's "love affair with the seventeenth century."[4]

Use of Edenic garden imagery and Adam's speech from *Paradise Lost* as well as mythical references and Christian symbolism give a religious sense to this modernistic novel of social isolation and alienation. Yet even more than that, in this early novel, psychological and spiritual language overlap, indicating they were connected in the mind of its young author. Writing a review in the *Cleveland Press,* Emerson Price perceptively notes:

> I found a deep and authentic exploration of the darker and more mystifying paths of human thought. . . . . all the half-truths ever spoken

> extended into truths, while the stealthy, cunning and always unspoken language of the mind had been made wholly articulate . . . . a tapestry so artistically woven and carefully integrated that the very core of life may be seen in its complex design. . . . . The pattern also clearly reveals and defines the true nature of sin: and it exposes the penalties for sin which, once set in motion, must involve saint and sinner alike. (24)

That the psychological "mystifying paths of human thought" and the "always unspoken language of the mind" would be used to speak about the "true nature of sin [which]. . . must involve saint and sinner alike" prefigures the psycho-spirituality of Buechner's later work. These psychological and spiritual interconnections in Buechner's first novel are present long before his conversion to Christianity in 1953 and his decision to attend Union Seminary.

Yet his perception is limited. Psychologically he paints the pain of isolation, inner woundedness, and fragmentation in the lives of these characters, but his remedy as exemplified by the wise grandmother Maroo is to become complete in herself and invulnerable. As she dies, she senses satisfaction in her influence on her grandson, Leander:

> So successfully had her hopes for him been realized, she understood, that he was invulnerable not only as far as the subtle perils of being alive were concerned, perils of which she had written him with quaint indirection in her letters, but as far as the source of his invulnerability, as far as herself, was concerned too. (262)

As Buechner matured, as a writer and a person, his spiritual sensibility expanded to accept rather than despair over human frailty. Though doubt and pessimism were never gone, they were not the last word. To embrace vulnerability and brokeness, the "strength made perfect in weakness" of his clay-footed saints, Buechner found a deeper personal experience of both psychotherapy and grace. This change occurred as Buechner grew in his psychological and spiritual understanding.

Buechner's second novel *The Seasons' Difference* (1952) contains the same critique of modernism present in *A Long Day's Dying*, but this time a counterbalancing theme is the importance of childlike faith and the possibility (though not certainty) of visionary experience. In terms of psychological manifestations from Buechner's own experience, it is interesting to note that as in the first novel, suicide casts a shadow over the events in the characters' lives. Prior to the beginning of the novel, Julie McMoon's husband has committed suicide. Because of this, she is an unbeliever who resists Cowley's search for a mystical vision. She admits her inner emptiness, and while playing hide and seek in the woods, thinks she sees her dead husband. Each character offers an explanation for what Julie saw. Psychological themes about seeing and believing, and seeing what one most hopes to see are played in varying tunes, with the final affirmation of Cowley's inner transformation, whether or not his vision was literal. On one side is Cowley's joyful yet irrational faith; on the other are the practical realists Dunn and Julie who reject the possibility of the miraculous. Dunn lives with his eyes closed (he literally sleeps through the children's reenactment of the "vision") and his refusal to believe precludes seeing a miracle even if it were to occur. Like the death of the wise matriarch in his first novel, *The Seasons' Difference* ends with the death of the grandfather figure: unwilling to stay in the cynical adult world of experience, the aged reverend seeks to join the children in their treehouse, where faith and innocence still live. Attempting the climb, he falls and dies. The stark choice of spirituality and mental imbalance vs rational control, cynicism (the Uglies) and human isolation seem the only alternatives available in a world of innocence and experience.

THE EARLY NOVELS: WHERE DREAMS COME FROM

Many critics dismissed this second novel as unrealistic and unconvincing. Sensitive to his harsher critics, Buechner increased his focus on psychology and the social gospel in his third novel, situated in the real world of emotional and material need and national politics.

The Return of Ansel Gibbs (1958), written while Buechner was in seminary and while traveling in Europe, is interesting in the ways he contains the overtly spiritual quest while amplifying the psychological themes. Responding in part to what Thomas Schaub calls "the liberal narrative," a disillusionment with ideology experienced by many liberal intellectuals after World War II, Buechner also tones down the emphasis on spiritual visionary experience which he tried to portray in *The Seasons' Difference*. Rather than write about possible mystical visions and childlike faith, Buechner seeks to focus instead on the ethical dilemmas and psychological conflicts of Ivy League intellectuals. This is closer to the modernist themes of alienation, ambivalence and inaction of his first novel, but unlike it, *The Return of Ansel Gibbs* suggests a possible psychological and spiritual resolution.

The central thematic focus is the protagonist's psychological struggle with ambivalence in the modern world. Asked his political position by reporters sent to query him as potential cabinet nominee, Ansel Gibbs verbalizes the dilemmas of the intellectual in the 1950s by explaining:

> ... to be civilized is to be aware of so many possible courses of action at any given time that no one of them ever seems to be without qualification right. Everything is qualified. Legal and ethical principles are good for today, but can't be rigidly fixed for tomorrow. (114)

In "The New Nihilism and the Novel," Norman Podhoretz discusses the loss of values in contemporary society as the theme in several American novels such as *The Return of Ansel Gibbs*:

> Civilization . . . means for Buechner a consciousness of the tragic ambivalence of life, and being civilized exerts a severe toll: Gibbs suffers from a certain deficiency of feeling.... He is almost incapable of passion (sobriety, judiciousness, detachment, moderation, tolerance being the civilized virtues). (576)

Stinging from the harsh reviews of *The Seasons' Difference*, Buechner focuses on more acceptable psychological issues. Spiritual issues are exemplified in the social gospel (Reverend Kuykendall's ministry with the poor in Harlem) and the inner struggles of an articulate man seeking to do the right thing ethically. Instead of debating mystical experience and faith, the nature of idealism and realism is examined.

Buechner has stated that his fiction comes from the same place dreams come from, and the underlying basis of the novel reflects the author's pain although he claimed it was not autobiographical. *The Return of Ansel Gibbs* concerns a father's suicide which heavily influences the dynamics in the other characters's lives, although it took place years before the novel begins. Rudy Tripp, the suicidal character, is an exact replica of Buechner's own father. We are told he had good looks and popularity as a young Ivy Leaguer who loved to swim and dance, he developed a growing sense of failure as he moved from job to job, he bid a silent farewell while the son played in his room early one morning, and he left a suicide note to his wife on the last page of *Gone With the Wind*, a best seller in 1936. The protagonist, Ansel Gibbs, feels guilt over his failure to prevent his friend's suicide, which occurred fifteen years before. Although he appears confident, Robin Tripp, the son of the dead man, has no real sense of self, having lost his father at such a young age and much of Buechner's own experience is presented in this character. Like Buechner's own mother, we are told that at the time of the suicide, Mrs. Tripp covered her ears and refused to talk about her husband's suicide when Ansel Gibbs had tried to offer condolences. When Buechner's mother read the novel, the thinly disguised details of the suicide left her feeling betrayed, and she was so angry she never read anything else her son wrote. At the time of writing a novel, Buechner is often not aware of the unconscious issues he expresses in his fiction. For example, when asked about the references to his father's suicide in an interview, Buechner claimed he was unlike Robin Tripp and had to rely purely on his imagination to guess what the son might have felt like if his father's suicide still bothered him.

As previously mentioned, the psychological dynamics of characters' past and present reflections are narrated by an omniscient third-person narrator who traces their development as they listen to their lives. Although Buechner himself had not yet been in therapy, for Ansel Gibbs, a time of deep thinking and realistically facing issues is the psychological solution, accompanied by the wise counsel of the Reverent Kuykendall and the support of family and friends. Both Ansel Gibbs and Robin Tripp come to admit their pain and woundedness, but there is no reference to counseling or psychotherapy, nor is the more spiritual "healing of memories" mentioned. But in dealing at length with the characters' anguish over Rudy Tripp's suicide, Buechner is showing that painful memories have repercussions and will have to be faced and overcome.

Spirituality is embodied in the character of Kuykendall, modeled after James Muilenburg, Buechner's Old Testament professor at Union Seminary (NT 35). Kuykendall is a wise, prophetic minister, serving the poor in Harlem, who utters verbatim many of Muilenburg's sayings. Unlike *The Seasons' Difference*, Buechner uses the non-mystical, articulate character of Kuykendall to address spiritual issues such as Gibbs' "call." Both Gibbs' and Kuykendall's idealism has been tempered by experience, and neither expects Gibbs to be a prophet with a vision. Simply to be himself, despite ambivalence and imperfection, is enough. Both spirituality and psychology have found a middle, less dramatic ground in this detached third-person narrative set in the mid-fifties during the McCarthy era when fanaticism and the Cold War made intellectuals skeptical of ideological solutions.

Whereas psychological themes characterize *The Return of Ansel Gibbs*, spiritual themes are central in Buechner's fourth novel, *The Final Beast* (1965), the first novel written after his ordination. Following his graduation from Union Seminary and ordination as a Presbyterian minister, Buechner became chaplain and head of the religion department at Phillips Exeter Academy. In selecting novels for his students to read, he realized:

> although many modern writers have succeeded in exploring the depths of human darkness and despair and alienation in a world where God seems largely absent, there are relatively few who have tried to tackle the reality of whatever salvation means, the experience of Tillich's New Being whereby, even in the depths, we are touched here and there by a power beyond power to heal and make whole. (NT 48)

Buechner decided that his next novel would be about "the presence of God rather than his absence . . . death and dark and despair as not the last reality but only the next to the last." (NT49). Taking a sabbatical leave during 1963-64, he wrote *The Final Beast*, a novel in which the separate realms of spirituality and psychology are articulated more clearly than in Buechner's previous fiction. Though it is an overtly religious book written about an ordained minister, the characterization and plot employ psychological innuendoes and revelations: Irma's painful memories of the concentration camp and her dreams, Nicolet's inner dilemmas and debates, Roonie Vail's mental anguish about her adultery and dreams, and even the psychological explanation of the Judas figure's motivation. As in his previous novels, the omniscient third-person narrator provides the reader with glimpses into the main characters' psyches. Yet the resolution for the psychological dilemmas the characters face is primarily spiritual, linked to the healing of memories through prayer and God's forgiveness.

Spiritual, literary, and psychological allusions overlap in the title *The Final Beast*. Buechner takes these words from a poem by Stephen Crane (quoted as the novel's epigraph) which from a naturalist point of view underscores the psychological determinism (the beasts) plaguing modern persons. But in Buechner's unique psychological-spiritual fashion, the "final beast" also comes from Revelation 19:19, a reference to the last beast which God will overthrow before bringing about a New Heaven and a New Earth. In spite of human tragedy, a positive psychological and spiritual outcome is possible for the Christian artist, as Amos Wilder observes: "In the toils of actual human perversity and malignancy the "final beast" . . . *is* sometimes overcome, and we *do* sometimes see the goodness of the Lord in the land of the living" (94).

The protagonist is a young minister pictured as sincere yet wavering in faith and somewhat foolish, with a clown's smile. This duality of his spirituality and his humanity is expressed in his name: Theodore (lover of God) Nicolet (alias "jolly St. Nick" a name given him in derision by the Judas figure Will Poteat). Nicolet recounts his conversion while hearing a moving sermon and has a mystical experience in nature hearing the "clack clack" of the branches, although he sees nothing miraculous with his eyes. Nicolet's spiritual experiences come from Buechner's own life (he records them in *Sacred Journey*) but this is not to say Nicolet is Buechner. Both are Protestant ministers, but Buechner does not face the same dilemmas confronting Nicolet, although as a young minister he can understand facing one's own doubts and failures.

The character Theodore Nicolet has intentional similarities with Graham Greene's whiskey priest in *The Power and the Glory*. Teaching Greene's novel at Exeter, Buechner became fascinated by the nameless little priest who felt himself a failure yet brought hope to his scattered parishioners and died a martyr. As Brown points out in "To Be a Saint: Frederick Buechner's *The Final Beast* and Rewriting Graham Greene," in Nicolet Buechner created a flawed, blundering, self-doubting priest who ministers in spite of himself like Greene's whiskey priest. Buechner's articulation of God's grace working through brokeness is also a paradox central to Christianity and psychotherapy. Only as a person admits failure and accepts the pain of past experiences can he or she be healed or be used to heal others (the wounded healer). In *The Final Beast*, however, Buechner articulates the need to go beyond purely psychological principles.

To do this he uses the character of Lillian Flagg, modeled after author and Episcopalian lay healer Agnes Sanford, whom Buechner met on a pastoral retreat. Like Sanford, Flagg prays for the healing of a person's memories, a kind of spiritual psychotherapy. In response to Rooney Vail's question about why she is childless though physically healthy, Lillian Flagg discerns her need for inner healing and forgiveness of sin:

> "People get hurt." ... "They hurt other people, and other people hurt them, things that happen hurt them. It locks doors inside a person—rooms and passages are shut off—and nothing in the world, nobody, can get in the darkness of those closed up places. No light and air, no life. Then it's not the healing of the body that has to happen. It's the healing of the memories. My dear, it's the forgiveness of sin." (50)

Here, through the character of Lillian Flagg, Buechner equates the healing of memories and the forgiveness of sin. Yet he clarifies that this healing requires more than human counseling. When Rooney asks how the healing can be accomplished, Flagg responds, "When it comes to sin, I'm afraid only God can stand the stench" (51). Following Flagg's suggestion, Rooney walks back through the "rooms" of her life (reliving her hurt trail), finally realizing the room that is closed: the painful memory of an adulterous sexual encounter. When she meets her pastor, she confesses this to him. Nicolet tries to offer "modern advice" by telling Rooney just to go back to her husband and forget her past adultery. In a private conversation, Lillian Flagg challenges Nicolet's humanistic approach:

> ". . . it's just the advice she'd want if she wanted advice. Only give her what she really wants, Nicolet."
> "Give her what, for Christ's sake?"
> "For Christ's sake . . ." Lillian Flagg took a deep breath, then let it out slowly, shaking her head. "The only thing you have to give." And then she almost shouted at him. "Forgive her for Christ's sake, little priest!"
> "But she knows I forgive her."
> "She doesn't know God forgives her. That's the only power you have—to tell her that. Not just that he forgives her the poor little adultery. But the faces she can't bear to look at now . . . . Tell her he forgives her for being lonely and bored, for not being full of joy with a houseful of children. That's what sin really is. You know—not being full of joy. Tell her that sin is forgiven because whether she knows it or not, that's what she wants more than anything else—what all of us want. What on earth do you think you were ordained for?" (95)

Like Greene's "little priest," despite his own failings, Nicolet carries out his spiritual calling, proclaiming God's forgiveness to Rooney and effecting a change in her life.

Buechner uses Agnes Sanford's metaphor of a house with

closed rooms to describe his own psychological condition in *Telling Secrets*. As he becomes aware of the closed rooms, he enters them by asking for help— not only through prayer and divine intervention but also through psychotherapy. However, at the time he wrote *Final Beast*, Buechner was just beginning to realize the dynamics of inner healing which in this novel comes through spiritual channels of faith healing and priestly intercession. Spiritual and psychological healing are not integrated at this point in his fiction, although the concept of healing memories relates to both.

The first book written by Buechner after his ordination, *The Final Beast* includes psychological references, but its main focus is on the need for spiritual renewal. For the first time Buechner was labeled a Christian novelist. In a 1965 review, Amos N. Wilder asked whether it is possible to be accepted as a writer with a Christian perspective by a modern reader:

> In Frederick Buechner's new novel, *The Final Beast,* we have a good test case of whether a modern artist can make traditional Christian language probable or palatable or effective to a general audience today. Can a novelist or playwright be unashamedly Christian in this sense, naively evangelical: can he deal directly with prayer, miracles, absolution without seeming preachy, without losing the secular reader or even the sophisticated Christian? (93)

Amos answered yes because "the evangelical formulas and behavior are located unmistakably in the midst of the world's business and obsessions" (93).

But many secular critics answered no. In a review of *The Final Beast* "Writing on cloth can be tricky," citing the literary tradition begun in Matthew Arnold's *Literature and Dogma* (1873), Julian Moynahan states:

The Early Novels: Where Dreams Come From

> from the standpoint of the priest and the standpoint of the writer, as, so to speak, primary producers, there is still a deep conflict between religion and literature.... They will "moralize this spectacle" differently because they have trained, or ought to have trained, their sensibilities differently. (6)
>
> Buechner binds character after character into the tight pattern of his fable of redemption and in the process violates their integrity as persons in a substantial fictional world.... The governing attitude of the *Final Beast* lodges itself uneasily at midpoint between the priest's and the writer's way of looking at things. (8)

Sensing the same conflict, the mixed review in the *Christian Science Monitor* (February 18, 1965) notes the "clash between a theological point of view and an artist's" but at the same time appreciates "the relentless honesty" of the protagonist and the creation of scenes of joy "like some of the joyous inventing in Fitzgerald." (A.W. Phinnery *Christian Science Monitor* February 18 1965).

Both *Time* and *Newsweek* dismissed the novel as religious propaganda. In a negative review entitled "Dove on Wires," *Newsweek* quipped, "In 1958, Buechner became a Presbyterian minister; and with *The Final Beast* he has written a ministerial sort of novel, a melodrama with theological overtones about two kinds of love—sacred and profane" (92). While many critics relegated it to the category of "religious fiction" and no longer took it seriously as literature, others such as the reviewer in the *Hudson Review* felt the novel was not Christian enough:

> One is so little convinced that Nicolet's faith exists as anything other than a rubber bone his ego can gnaw on when it gets hungry, that the

religious aspect of his character, which is presumably central, merely serves to add a prurient flavor of theological titillation to his sexual yearning for Rooney. The prurience, which is surely inadvertent, comes from Mr. Buechner's reluctance to think at all seriously about his subject. (Green 285)

Buechner was stung by the negative critical reaction for he had included his own spiritual experience in *The Final Beast.*

Most critics faulted Buechner's overt handling of spiritual issues which they felt was heavy-handed. Those who favored the novel appreciated both its religious emphasis and the ambivalence of the protagonist. For example, in the *Saturday Review*, Chester E. Eisinger wrote,

> *The Final Beast*, offering a religious interpretation of contemporary American experience, expands our areas of consciousness and widens the perspectives of the American novel ... a genuine contribution to the serious fiction of faith.

While noting the negative reaction Buechner's Christian subject matter would cause, John Davenport, in *The Spectator,* stated, "His novel is a minor masterpiece of wit and human understanding." The American Library Association included it in the list of fifty-one "Notable Books of 1965" (Flannery O'Connor's posthumous short stories collection *Everything That Rises Must Converge* was also included). When almost twenty years later *The Final Beast* was republished by Harper and Row, John Mellin, the reviewer in *Theology Today,* captured the nature of the critical debate over Buechner's handling of spiritual issues:

THE EARLY NOVELS: WHERE DREAMS COME FROM

> Frederick Buechner, clergyman novelist, has been rediscovered through his most recently published theological works . . Too religious for secular critics and too secular for religious critics . . . . Of all Buechner's novels this one faces most authentically the religious concerns of his recent non-fiction. The issue of redemption is woven into the contemporary American experience in a realistic and honest way. . . . It is as if Harper & Row has republished this novel as an illustration of the non-fiction works. Buechner fans will love it. (103)

From this point on, many intellectual Christian readers eagerly awaited anything Buechner wrote, seeking validation for a Christian perspective at the hands of a skillful literary writer. The sacred and secular camps became polarized around the issue of Buechner as a "Christian novelist." Part of the problem for non-believing readers was that they could not identify with the protagonist, even though he expressed conflicts and doubts. Buechner seemed to have minimized his psychological approach in favor of the spiritual.

Even before his conversion and ordination, Buechner was mixing modernist themes with Christian references, a factor not noted by the critics who divided Buechner's writings into BC and AD, citing the two modernist novels written before his conversion, while the "Christian novels" came afterwards. W. Dale Brown, who has emphasized the consistency of Buechner's themes of doubt and ambivalence throughout his writings, notes this mistaken approach:

> Critics have often broken Frederick Buechner's career into two parts. The phenomenally successful first book, *A Long Day's Dying*, and the less successful *The Seasons'*

Difference are placed on one side. Then come conversion and ordination, to be followed by forty years of books written directly from a Christian consciousness. Such a view unfortunately reduces the spiritual longing in the early books and the struggles for faith in the more recent ones. (*Of Fiction and Faith* 31)

Most academic scholars such as Myers, Brown, Engbers, Bruinooge, and Horton Davies emphasize the counterpointal themes of faith and doubt, grace and ambivalence running throughout the entire Buechner corpus. In contrast to simplistic Christian reductionism, Brown focuses on the continuing questions and doubt that plague Buechner's most spiritual protagonists—be they Nicolet, Godric, or Leo Bebb. Myers stresses the poetic quality running throughout the corpus which "is used to convey the introspective, intensely self-conscious state of mind of the characters, a state of mind that is conducive to spiritual awareness." (8) This parallels my thesis that Buechner uses psychological and spiritual insights to portray a character actively listening to his or her life. Prior to his use of a first-person narrator, these concepts were not fully explored or articulated, especially in his fiction. As explained in Chapter Two, this did not occur until Buechner spontaneously articulated what it meant to listen to his life in his autobiographical journal *Alphabet of Grace*.

Buechner's earliest novels prefigure his later psychological and spiritual developments. The modernism of *Long Day's Dying* portrays unfilled spiritual longings through psychological introspection, ambivalent vacillation, miscommunication and isolation. *The Return of Ansel Gibbs* weaves credible spiritual insights into the psychological struggles of a modern protagonist who comes to accept himself and the forgiveness and support of his community, leading him away from isolation and into the arena of political involvement and self-actualization. *The Final Beast* portrays the need for spiritual healing for psychological and spiritual weakness. Written from the perspective of a third-person omniscient narrator, spiritual and psychological struggles of characters in the early novels overlap, prefiguring the more compelling ways they will appear in *The Book of Bebb*, *Godric*, and *Son of Laughter* as Buechner develops a deeper understanding of listening to his life, through autobiography, therapy, and spirituality.

Buechner's growing psychological understanding comes through his later novels. Beginning therapy in the 1970s, his insights become psychologically attuned with a universal resonance. As Allen reiterates, that which is most personal is most universal. It is not that Buechner now consciously applies a more articulate psychological paradigm in his writing. Rather it is because the author himself has changed that the writing is more alive. Having experienced in therapy what it means to be a wounded healer, Buechner embodies in his characters the psychological and spiritual emphasis of narrative theology and psychotherapy. These techniques alone do not make great literature, but in the hands of a superb writer, polyphonic dialogue, the intuitive feel for character, plus a deep understanding of the self, provide the rich soil in which a master craftsman can create. It is not the themes, or the psychology, or the spirituality, per se, but the ways Buechner is able to combine these with a fertile imagination to touch a deep resonance with readers.

Notes

1 In her 1976 dissertation "Sanctifying the Profane: Religious Themes in the Fiction of Frederick Buechner," Nancy B. Myers groups Buechner's novels chronologically into his three stylistic developments: "His first novels, *A Long Day's Dying* (1950), *The Seasons' Difference* (1952), and *The Return of Ansel Gibbs* (1958) are composed in a baroque, elegant style that is often referred to as 'Jamesian.' *The Final Beast* (1965) and *The Entrance to Porlock* (1970) are in a more relaxed, whimsical, comic mode. From 1971 to 1974 Buechner produced a trilogy, *Lion Country*, *Open Heart*, and *Love Feast*, which demonstrate a new, freer style—colloquial, breezy, and even ribald." (2)

2 After his experience in therapy, he would describe the defenses Adam and Eve seek to hide behind as an inappropriate way to deal with inner conflict.

3 In the classical myth of Tereus, Procne and Philomela, a tragic story of rape and deceit, the three characters are turned into birds by the gods. This myth was also used by T.S. Eliot in *The Waste Land* to portray the bankruptcy of modern relationships.

4 Buechner wrote his senior thesis "Notes on the Function of Metaphor in English Poetry" drawing heavily on the writings of Shakespeare, Milton, and Donne, as well as contemporary poets such as Auden, Yeats, and Stevens.

4

The Book of Bebb: Psychology and Spirituality Personified

I was reading a magazine as I waited my turn at a barber shop one day when, triggered by a particular article and the photographs that went with it, there floated up out of some hitherto unexplored subcellar of me a character who was to dominate my life as a writer for the next six years and more. He was a plump, bald, ebullient southerner who had once served five years in a prison on a charge of exposing himself before a group of children and was now the head of a religious diploma mill in Florida and of a seedy, flat-roofed stucco church called the Church of Holy Love, Incorporated. He wore a hat that looked too small for him. He had a trick eyelid that every once in a while fluttered shut on him. His name was Leo Bebb. (NT 97)

What was there about Bebb that engaged me so? Part of what seems to happen in dreams—and what makes them sometimes prophetic—is

> that in them you live out parts of yourself that have not yet entered your waking life either because you have never consciously recognized them or because for one reason or another you have chosen not to. (NT 99)

In *The Book of Bebb* psychology and spirituality are dynamically juxtaposed through the diverse perspectives of the two main characters. Especially in the first novel *Lion Country*, the narrator Antonio Parr embodies psychological reductionism. Constantly introspective, he listens to his life through obsessive introspection and Freudian analysis. Dreams, Freudian slips, phallic symbols, projection, transference are all part of his way of perceiving reality. In contrast, Leo Bebb gives a spiritual interpretation to everything that happens. He quotes scripture, chapter and verse. He talks about prayer and the will of the Lord. As these two characters who seem poles apart begin to interact, their psychological and spiritual ways of listening to life begin to overlap. Antonio begins to turn his self-analysis into a spiritual quest, and Bebb shares psychological insights into how to deal with a painful past, although he cannot always follow his own advice.

Exposure—physical, psychological and spiritual— affects both characters. Bebb has been arrested for indecent exposure, an act which indicates an even deeper shame. For Bebb, the psychological scars of the past have created emotional deficits which need psychological as well as spiritual healing. Parr fears exposure, risk and commitment. He wishes to remain hidden behind his false self of psychological cynicism. Through self-exposure and exposure to the life force in Bebb, Parr becomes receptive to the spiritual. At the same time Bebb's psychological needs become increasingly apparent as he again sexually exposes himself during an ordination service. Thus Buechner uses insights from psychology to create a very human, fallible character in Leo Bebb. At the same time, the psychological introspections of Antonio Parr are counterproductive until he realizes his false self is being exposed and he begins to see the meaning of his life in spiritual terms.

Buechner's psychological and spiritual concerns are thus vividly expressed through the interaction of these two protagonists, for Antonio Parr embodies modern psychological reductionism and Bebb embodies old-fashioned religious faith. They also embody dual sides of Buechner, the intuitive writer, who in creating them is living out unconscious parts of himself (NT 99). Parr and Bebb represent the psychological and spiritual struggles going on inside their author. Because Buechner himself is the skeptic and the true believer, he is able to cry and laugh with both.

Buechner identifies with Leo Bebb or would like to. In discussing what attracted him to Bebb, he explains how in some literary creations, like dreams "you live out parts of yourself that have not yet entered your waking life." He continues:

> Bebb was strong in most of the places where I was weak, and mad as a hatter in most of the places where I was all too sane. Bebb took terrible risks with his life where I hung back with mine and hoped no one would notice. In more ways than literally, Bebb was continually exposing himself, coming right out and telling it the way it was .... Bebb's doubts were darker and more painful than mine because he had grown up knowing more of pain and darkness, and that made his faith both a kind of crazy miracle in itself and a faith also that could work miracles.
>
> Life was, above all else, the miracle that Bebb worked, I think, because in one preposterous, Bebbsian way or another he made life burn a little hotter and brighter in all the people who came his way in those four novels and most certainly in myself as well who both brought him into being and was in certain ways, in certain aspects,

> brought into being with him.... Maybe it was by a good deal more than just luck that he floated up into my consciousness that day. Maybe our most life-giving and prophetic dreams are always more than just luck. In any case, it was from Bebb that I learned to be braver about exposing myself and my own story as I have both in this present book and in *The Sacred Journey*. I feel sure that, for better or worse, neither of them could have been written without him. (NT 100-101)

One key to unlocking Buechner's psychology and spirituality and his relationship to his two protagonists is his use of a first-person narrator. This stylistic technique allows him to create a sense of spontaneity as he writes in the first person, becoming a character who listens to his life. As Buechner has stated in the opening sentence of *Alphabet of Grace*: "At its heart most theology like most fiction, is essentially autobiography" (3). In 1969 Buechner began thinking about his experience of seeing God's activity in the details of everyday life as an alphabet of grace. His autobiographical journal marked a new articulation of his approach to spirituality, made possible by his use of a first-person narrator. After completing *Alphabet of Grace*, Buechner began a novel using a similar spontaneous, self-revealing first-person narrator to fashion one of his most powerful expressions of psychological and spiritual interactions: *Lion Country*.

In discussing the process of creating *Lion Country*, which was so much more spontaneous than his previous novels, "a process much less of invention than of discovery" (NT 98), Buechner states that for the first time as a novelist

> I used the device of a first-person narrator, and although Antonio Parr was by no means simply myself in thin disguise—our lives had been very different; we had different personalities,

> different ways of speaking—just to have a person telling his own story in a rather digressive, loose-jointed way was extremely liberating to me as a writer. For the first time I felt free to be funny in ways that I hadn't felt comfortable being in print before, to let some of my saltier-tongued characters use language that before had struck me as less than seemly in a serious work of fiction, to wander off into quirkish reminiscences and observations that weren't always directly related to my central purpose. . . . But there was also something much more than just that, and what it was, supremely and without any question, was Bebb himself. (NT 98-99)

Although Bebb is the central character in many ways, the story is told entirely from the perspective of Antonio Parr, the humorously skeptical narrator. Written as an autobiographical memoir of his interactions with Leo Bebb, Parr's narratorial style is more reminiscent of a spontaneous Woody Allen monologue than the carefully crafted, third-person narration of Buechner's earlier novels. As a sophisticated New Yorker, Parr offhandly gives psychological interpretations to his introspective musings and the events of everyday life. A perceptive observer, he often recounts the utterances of the other characters verbatim. Unlike some of the characters in the earlier novels, who tended to be embodiments of ideas, the characters in *The Book of Bebb* are living persons with distinct voices and authentic, though outlandish, personalities. From the quirky and humorous viewpoint of Antonio Parr to which the reader is privy, they are also comic and engaging.

Having seen an article about a Southern preacher arrested for indecent exposure, Buechner spontaneously began to write *Lion Country*, the first novel in what was to become a tetralogy, *The Book of Bebb*. The novel was completed in less than three months, received critical acclaim in the popular press and was nominated for the 1971 National Book award. In his introduction to *The Book of Bebb* (1979), published as a one-volume tetralogy composed of *Lion Country* (1971), *Open Heart* (1972), *Love Feast* (1974), and *Treasure Hunt* (1977), Buechner describes his unusual experience of writing the first novel in the series:

> From wherever it is that dreams come from, a whole world rose up for me more or less on the spot . . . . when I started out, I don't think I had any very clear idea where I was going. I know I had some notion of making Bebb a villain, but almost from the beginning I could see that wasn't going to work. Antonio Parr was going to expose him for the charlatan we both thought he was, but then it became apparent that Antonio Parr himself was the one who was going to get exposed. . . .
> (BB vii-viii)

Instead of starting first with an idea or a modernist dilemma, this novel began with a central character, a new narrative technique, and the mysterious creative process by which a "whole world which rose up for me on the spot." Buechner's unconscious resources were being stirred. Immediately, the style, humor, and spirit of the book engaged readers. His vivid characterizations were universally recognized by critics:

> Buechner has always been an important novelist, but his characters previously seemed vague and remote. . . . In [*Lion Country*] Buechner grasps each figure firmly . . . . causing them to pop out almost fully alive from the novel. . . . [It] is an impressive book—and an important book. Each rereading evokes more meaning and thought . . . . It is Buechner's finest work so far,

and that is saying much because his other novels are significant and vital. (Doyle 54)

Critics who six years earlier dismissed *The Final Beast* as religious propaganda, now praised the Bebb novels for their comic yet powerful depictions of characters and spiritual issues. *Newsweek* called *Lion Country*

> Frederick Buechner's sixth novel and his best ...an ordained Presbyterian minister... [he] has turned upon sacred matters a most wonderfully secular, often profane, fancy... Buechner enriches every character with the vital comic potential of Bebb and the stoic grace of Miriam. (*Newsweek* Feb. 22, 1971 96)

In a light-hearted comparison to Graham Greene's *Power and the Glory*, *Life* magazine included *Lion Country* in its "Reviewers choice" stating that

> The market isn't what it used to be, but if you insist on becoming a religious novelist, be a Catholic... you simply can't beat those drinking priests, those burnt-out cases. By comparison, the Protestant Graham Greenes seem to be dealing with traffic tickets. [But] Frederick Buechner, a Presbyterian minister and a superb stylist, has done his best to close the Sin Gap. (*Life* April, 1971)

James Dickey wrote, "Frederick Buechner is one of our finest writers . . . *Lion Country* is surely his best book to date," an assessment repeated by Louis Auchincloss and many other critics.

Here the psychological themes of human weakness find expression in the "saint" and the "sinner," who are both exposed.

Cynthia Ozick called this "sanctifying the profane." In the *New York Times Book Review* she writes,

> ... Buechner is, by his own lights and in some of the most masterly comic prose being written in America, sanctifying the profane. Fraud is only a seeming; suffering and frailty are the means of our purification, and death is not death but eternal life. (4)

Although Ozick praised the novel, her review oversimplified Buechner's handling of the spiritual issues and overlooked the character changes and psychological nuances. Her statement that Buechner was "sanctifying the profane"[1] has particular merit, however, especially when applied to the ways he sanctifies psychological insights by exploring their spiritual implications.

The reader's view of Bebb and the other characters is filtered through the eyes of Antonio Parr. Parr personifies the modernist anti-hero, whose wryly humorous comments and psychoanalytic perspective reflect that of a contemporary audience. In his introduction to the tetralogy, Buechner describes Parr as "an olive-skinned young drifter and introvert who looked a little like the young J.D. Salinger" (vii). Parr's narrative voice is effective for he is both transparent and perceptive. Like Salinger's first-person narrator Holden Caulfield, he "sees the deep human need within even the most unpleasant people who wander through his life" (Buechner statement in Brown interview 46). Parr's doubt, ambivalence and inability to act are handled with such deft humor that the effect is comic rather than morose.

Parr is convincing as a character because he reflects the skeptical side of Buechner. In "Frederick Buechner and the Strange Work of Grace" Horton Davies stresses

> the profound understanding Buechner demonstrates in all his writings for the skeptic and

> for the cogency of that viewpoint. Buechner is able to do this because he was there himself for many years.... Buechner found great comfort in Paul Tillich's statement that doubt is not the opposite of faith, but an integral part of faith. This is shown in two ways in Buechner's novels.
>
> First, there is always a devil's advocate whose cynicism is a foil to any tendency there might be to adopt a canary-chirping optimism that ignored sin, suffering, and death. Secondly, the characters motivated by religion are also subject to the ambiguities of human existence. (187)

Both devil's advocate and fallible religious characters are seminal in the Bebb novels. Urbane, sophisticated, and witty, the skeptical Antonio Parr is a natural devil's advocate whose continual self-examination parallels Buechner's earlier alienated protagonists. As Buechner's narrator, Parr stands in a unique position to give voice to intellectually sophisticated cynicism as it encounters the evangelical fervor of Leo Bebb.

At the same time, right from the beginning, Bebb is a fallible hero, and Parr's goal is to expose the hypocrite and charlatan he believes him to be. These two characters respectively embody the psychological and spiritual perspectives which move from confrontation to wary acceptance, mutual respect, and even love.

Parr's ingrained psychological approach comes through his characteristic skepticism, articulated in terms his introspection and self-analysis. Constantly examining his own inner motivation, relationships and dreams, Parr views the world through Freudian glasses. He speculates about repressed oedipal conflicts, sexual symbolism, and hidden neurotic conflicts. While sometimes being a psychological defense, this approach has another side, for the same awareness of unconscious motivations provides the basis for Parr's openness to the mysterious spiritual dimension at work in Leo Bebb. Thus the psychological and spiritual begin to come together in the character of Antonio Parr, the narrator with whom most readers would identify in his struggles to find his identity and create lasting relationships.

Parr's quasi-Freudian perspective adds humor while acting as a defense against facing spiritual issues most strongly in *Lion Country*, the Bebb novel in which Buechner's psycho/spiritual technique is most pronounced. For example, when his dying twin sister is contemplating life after death, Parr bypasses her questions with Freudian sarcasm, which she recognizes as a hollow defense.

> "The queerest thing is this feeling I have I'm *going* someplace," she said, "instead of just out, like a match. I should have been a better Catholic. Maybe I'd understand more. All last night I kept dreaming about doors opening."
>
> "Vaginas," I said. "I thought everybody knew that."
>
> She said, "Listen, I'm through with that stuff for good" (BB 8)

"That stuff" is the obsequious Freudian interpretations so commonplace in the 1950s and 60s in the United States. Interpreting dreams as symbolic masks for repressed conflicts had become a commonplace, and sexual implications of phallic symbols were so accepted in public discourse that jokes were often made by implication. (Sometimes a cigar is just a cigar.) Previously Miriam had expressed concern about her two sons being cared for by her ex-husband and his housekeeper whom she describes in Freudian terms:

> "The castrating mother—I mean *her*—and the castrated father. I'm scared to death they're going to turn those boys into fairies" (21).

Miriam's later response to Antonio when she is nearing death indicates, however, that she is no longer content with pseudo-science and is now facing the ultimate questions without defense or pretense. This interplay of Freudian and spiritual interpretation is often juxtaposed in *Lion Country*, especially in Parr's focus on dreams.

Dreams, and their possible interpretations, are significant throughout the novel, and as narrator, Parr often recalls his dreams, which he accepts as relating to levels of his conscious and unconscious thoughts. For example, on the overnight train from New York to Armadillo, Florida, he recounts three dreams reflecting increasingly deeper levels of consciousness.

In this first dream, Parr dreams of a girl (whom he had just met on the train) lying in the hospital, with a blank where her face should have been. When she reaches out her hand, it becomes a fishhook, reminiscent of Parr's recent traumatic experience with his cat. This dream seems to be a jumbled composite of his recent experiences, and shows that his sister in the hospital is very much on his mind.

In the second dream he is riding on a train with his father, who died when he was twelve. In the dream, however, the father is alive and apparently "had never actually died at all. It had been just some complicated misunderstanding" (27). This dream gives the feeling that Antonio is trying to come to grips with death, loss and his past. In recounting the dream, he is surprised to learn he is still affected by the death of his father which took place twenty-two years before. His relationship to his father long forgotten has been repressed and is now being expressed in the form of a dream.

The third dream on the train is the most significant. Parr states:

> But the dream I remember most vividly and that for obvious reasons disturbed me most took place on a stretch of tropical beach which I recognized somehow as Armadillo. Chris and Tony, my two young nephews, were there. . .

.They were dressed in dark suits, and I realized they must have come down for their mother's funeral.... I was standing in front of them dressed also for a funeral, and their gaze was fixed steadily upon me. Little by little I was undressing. First I took off my tie and jacket, then my shirt, my socks and shoes and trousers, so that finally I had nothing on but my undershorts. . . . .

After a while the boys stood up woodenly as though to sing a hymn or at the entrance of the priest, and at that point I dropped my undershorts and stood there completely naked with their solemn dark eyes watching me... I felt something unspeakable happening to me and cried out to them, "See me! See me!" as though my life depended on it, or perhaps what I cried out was "Semen! Semen!" (27)

On one level, the explicit sexual nature of the dream manifests Freudian notions of repression and conflict; on a literary level this dream is particularly significant because self-exposure is a central theme in *Lion Country*. Antonio Parr answers Bebb's newspaper ad in order to expose him as a religious charlatan. When he meets him to gain information for this exposé, he finds the tables turned when Bebb begins to analyze him:

> He (Bebb) said, "Antonio, I'm commencing to get the feel of you a little. You've had me doing most of the talking, but I've been watching your face and your eyes and they've told me many things —*more* things," he had a way of interrupting himself as if taking you down through deeper and deeper levels always nearer to some remarkable truth, "*maybe*," he interrupted again, taking me yet another step nearer, "more things than maybe

> you'd ever dream of telling me yourself." Whereupon I had the eerie sensation for a moment that I who was there to expose him was on the point of being exposed myself as being there under pretenses so false as to border on the supernatural. (9-10)

Although Bebb does not use psychological language, he assumes the role of a prophet/therapist who sees beneath the surface of the false self to expose what is hidden within.

This theme of exposure takes on a literal reality when Antonio reads an account of Bebb's previous arrest for indecent exposure. Learning of this act, Parr's response is outrage because in spite of his earlier suspicions, he had begun to trust Bebb, to develop "a therapeutic transference" after their first meeting. To describe his sense of betrayal, he plays on the word exposure:

> No exposure could have been more indecent than that of my own trusting innocence. When I discovered from the *Journal-American* that the case was indeed quite otherwise, I felt that I, the would-be betrayer, had been betrayed (15-16)

Despite his displaced anger, which will be discussed later, Parr realizes he is the one being exposed. This is underscored by his vivid dream on the train to Armadillo that he is exposing himself in front on nephews—shouting "see me, see me." Bebb's literal self-exposure and Antonio's psychological exposure is symptomatic of the universal human condition, in hiding to prevent exposure. In the hospital when Parr takes his nephews to say goodbye to their dying mother for the last time, he realizes they are all naked and don't have words to cover themselves, "those few moments when we sat there with nothing but silence to hide our nakedness behind.... [until] we found that we all had words to wear again and familiar parts to play in their familiar garb" (85).

All human beings play roles, assuming false selves to hide their inner hurt selves. Words can reveal but they can also be used as a defense, as they are here.

Hiding nakedness, covering up who one really is, is seen as a psychological defense. As discussed in chapter one, in his definition of "Psychotherapy" in *Whistling in the Dark: A Doubter's Dictionary*, Buechner uses the analogy of Adam and Eve trying to hide their nakedness before God. Aware of their nakedness and experiencing shame as a result of their alienation/sin, they try to hide and cover themselves with leaves, defenses of their own making. Only when they come out of hiding, face themselves as they are and receive God's provision (skins of animals) to cover their nakedness, are they free to move on. Thus facing their naked state is an essential step in the journey toward healing and wholeness, the same dynamic that is the basis of psychotherapy.

Bebb's propensity for indecent exposure, which occurs in *Lion Country* as part of his shameful past and is repeated during what should be the highpoint of his career (the ordination of the wealthy Indian chief Herman Redpath), has an underlying psychological and spiritual significance. When his daughter Sharon asks Bebb why he exposed himself in front of the congregation, he answers in terms implying Freudian accidental slips, wish fulfillment, and the exposing of deeper levels of the unconscious. Spiritually, it represents the confession of sin.

> He said, "Sharon honey, it was one of those things that happens, that's all it was. A accident." He said, "It was," then interrupting himself with one finger raised, "it wasn't a accident exactly. How you want to say? You might call it something on the order of—" and as he kept breaking in on himself, I thought, it was as if he was taking Sharon and himself too always down, down, to some deeper subcellar still of whatever might be the truth of it, some lower, urine-smelling level of the IRT.

> He said, "Time comes a man wants to be known for what he is, the bad with the good of him, the weakness with the strength. He wants to lay the whole shebang out in the light of day where the sun can get at it and folks can see all the shameful, hurtful parts of him same as the other parts that's decent and straight." (113)

The scene ends in the blaze of the noonday sun, when without his usual winking, Bebb sings, "Rock of Ages, cleft for me.... Let me hide myself in thee... Nothing in my hand I bring, Simply to thy cross I cling" (114). Bebb has exposed his nakedness (which we later learn represents an earlier adultery), is now in the light, and is seeking refuge in God's provision. Bebb has given up his own defenses by coming out of hiding. Thus exposed, he now "hides" himself in Christ, the Rock of Ages. In so doing he is "walking in the light." Buechner paints this picture of spiritual truth using the tacky symbolism of Bebb's church when with wry humor Parr adds, "... over his head, I noticed, almost too good to be true,...the light in the frosted-glass sign so that even in the daylight it shone out a little with HOLY LOVE written up and down it like the cross on a Bayer aspirin tablet" (114).

In psychotherapy, exposing the past is important so one can accept it and move on. Speaking with the wisdom of a therapist, Bebb describes the problems people make for themselves by not letting go of the past as scripture suggests they should.

> I don't hold a man's past against him any more than Jesus did. Remember the good thief, Antonio. Remember the woman taken in adultery. But there's people like Brownie that hold their own past against themselves till it gets where they can't break loose out of it any more. (94)

Lavern Brown, alias "Brownie," is Bebb's effeminate self-deprecating assistant, a timid soul, afraid of risk and the errors of the past. He has drawn back from life, even though he believes Bebb literally raised him from the dead. Brownie is always trying to please others; he is codependent, a "brown nose" unable to stand up for himself. Brownie literally lacks teeth; he has a permanent "china smile" of false teeth. Similarly, he takes the "bite" out of any unpleasant or difficult passages of Scripture, reinterpreting and sugar coating them to "make the rough places smooth." In this regard he is a forerunner of the monk Reginald, who seeks to sanctify Godric's life story to fit a saint's hagiography.

Two other characters, Bebb's wife Lucille and his brother Babe, are destroyed by their refusal to give up the past. Lucille (whose name ironically means light) cannot forgive herself for the murder of their child. An alcoholic, she wears dark glasses because "the light hurts her eyes," and in *Open Heart* she kills herself because she can no longer live with the past and fears being exposed. In *Treasure Hunt*, the last novel of the series, we meet Bebb's twin brother Babe who is described as "[Bebb] all over with the Gospel left out" (447). Named Babe by his brother even though he was the older twin, Babe cannot forgive Leo and his wife for their sexual encounter. Consumed with revenge and pathological jealousy, he dons disguises to commit crimes blamed on his wife so she will be isolated from the surrounding community. Babe becomes obsessed with space aliens while watching for Bebb's return. Thus Babe is controlled by the past and awaits escape in the future, but he is unable to live in the present.

Rather than covering over or hiding the past, exposure and confession involve truthful recognition and forgiveness of past mistakes. There is an acceptance of the past and future, rather than trying to escape or being consumed by them. Thus exposure leads to release and healing. Learning from the past through personal observation, psychotherapy, or spiritual awareness is what Buechner calls listening to one's life. Through introspection, Antonio Parr learns to see his life's meaning by trial and error. As he looks back over the events of his life he begins to see the alphabet of grace, starting with the letter A:

> Down and then up again, south and then north again. If these events in my life had a pattern, it was something like that.... .an upside-down A, I suppose, with the little bar in between representing the bridge that always connects the present with both the past and the future. Because when I was on my way down in my roomette as Tono, I had in me already seeds of the Antonio I was to become; and when I finally went up again with Sharon as my bride, I carried as part of my baggage and will carry always the celibate dabbler in unwelded scrap iron that I had been on the way down. (128)

Connected with a recognition and acceptance of the past, names in Buechner are significant as hallmarks of identity and represent another aspect of Buechner's psycho-spirituality. As in the Bible, names in Buechner's novels signify a character's psychological and spiritual development. In the earlier novels, the names Tristram Bone and Theodore Nicolet represent each protagonist's dual, conflicted identity. In *The Book of Bebb*, the protagonist's evolving name reflects inner character changes, as is seen in the later novels (Deric become Godric and Heels becomes Israel). As "Tono" the narrator is a 34-year-old bachelor who is unwilling to make a commitment. Everything he does is temporary, be it his "scrap iron" sculpture, which he does not weld in place, so it can be continuously rearranged, or his non-vital, uncommitted relationship with his girlfriend, or his ever changing professions. As Tono he is unwilling even to promise his dying twin sister he will look after her boys. Tono is his childhood name, a name that later his wife refuses to call him because it reminds her of "the baby word for number two."

Like his name, Tono's actions convey his incomplete development. Rather than take a plane to Armadillo, Tono prefers the train because it represents detachment, a decathexis (emotional detachment from life) to which he is prone:

> ... nobody can get at you in a train. You are in the world but not of it as you flash by as free and impermanent as the silver meteor for which my train that day was named." (20)
>
> It is what I like about trains. You are neither here nor there, and you a neither this nor that. You are in between. I mean in between not just in a geographical sense, of course, but like an actor waiting in the wings for his cue to re-enter, or a disembodied spirit drifting between incarnations like an unconfirmed rumor. Who you were last and who you are going to be next hardly matter. The drifting is all. (23)

He is Tono with his sister in New York and on the train. With Bebb, however, his name is Antonio, and upon meeting him, Bebb gets right to the point of his identity. Bebb tells him "I am here to save your soul, Antonio Parr. What kind of a name do you call that anyway?" (5).

Over the course of the novel, Parr grows into the name Bebb calls him. As a lapsed Catholic, he mentions his namesake, St. Anthony, the finder of lost things. He is a lost person, but as he assumes his identity as Antonio, he begins to function with more maturity. From cynicism, he gradually moves toward faith. From drifter without a title or profession, he becomes "the Reverend Antonio Parr," as he signs his name in the motel, in jest, but as a foretaste of what he is becoming. By the end of the novel he has married Bebb's daughter, taken responsibility for the boys after Miriam's death, and returned to a stable job teaching high-school English. The changes in his identity occur in pieces, with setbacks, but overall there is a growing sense of permanence and transcendence in his life.

In addition to Antonio Parr, the name Leo Bebb is significant for a protagonist who is identified with lions. He takes after the "plump, ebullient king named Rinkitink" (SJ 16) from the Wizard of Oz, who is both a foolish and wise king. Leo Bebb is a natural leader and a follower of Jesus, the "King of Kings." While amused by his ridiculous Happy Hooligan appearance, Parr gains respect for Bebb when they visit his favorite place, a wild game reserve called Lion Country, where lions roam about freely. Without any fear, Bebb walks out among the beasts, much like Daniel in the lion's den. Traditionally the lion, king of the jungle, represents courage, boldness and in *Lion Country*, freedom and natural power. Like Aslan in C. S. Lewis's *Chronicles of Narnia*, the lion symbolizes Christ, descendant of King David, Lion of the tribe of Judah. Leo Bebb shares the qualities of his namesake in his boldness, courage, freedom, and risk taking. He may also be a Christ figure.

The changes embodied in Antonio Parr's evolving identity are subtly foreshadowed from his first encounter with Bebb. Bebb's newspaper ad offering ordination certificates provokes Tono's introspective analysis of his mixed reaction to the ad:

> *Put yourself on God's payroll:* this burning bush tucked in among the hemorrhoid cures and dashboard Virgins and neckties that glowed in the dark. At every level I could have been held accountable on, it struck me as inspired rascality ripe for my exposing—except that I can believe now that in some subterranean way I may have been interested not only in exposing it but also perhaps in, shall we say, sampling it. At least I remember that when I received my ordination certificate and with it license to bury and marry, I found myself almost right away wondering crazily

> who and where and when. The Reverend Antonio Parr, I thought. The Peculiarly Reverend, the Preposterously Reverend Parr. (5-6)

Psychological workings of the unconscious on various levels are always significant in Parr's introspective analysis of his behavior. "At every level I could have been held accountable on" involves Parr's ethical, economic, and logical level of perception and consciousness. "Some subterranean way" implies the underlying unconscious impulses or even providential spiritual prompting which are equally significant but would only later be understood.

Parr often speculates about his inner motivation with specific reference to Freudian interpretations. This is particularly true in his relationships with women. Twice he speaks of his unwillingness to tell his twin sister about his romantic interests, wondering if it is because he is subconsciously dealing with the oedipal/incest taboo.

> I could never speak to one [woman] about the other without twinges of guilt. And the reason, I suppose, is that with both of them I was more than a little in love. (17)
>
> What I wanted to describe most to her, of course, was Sharon . . .but partly because the nurse kept coming in and out, and partly because for reasons that I suppose Dr. Freud would have found interesting I never was much good at telling Miriam about the women in my life. (117)

Mythological references also abound throughout the book to give both a spiritual and a psychoanalytic level of meaning to the story. Freud used analogies to the classical descent into the underworld to describe exploring the deeper realms of the unconscious.[2] Similarly, on the first page of *Lion Country*, Antonio describes his first vivid memory of Leo Bebb descending into the New York City subway like Orpheus:

The Book of Bebb: Psychology and Spirituality Personified

> Bebb descends to them [the characters he left behind in Armadillo] like Orpheus with his lyre, and in the dark they reach out their hands to him while up there at the entrance to the underworld I also reached out my hands (3).

Orpheus was so gifted in music he could charm the monsters guarding the underworld and bring back his wife Eurydice from the land of the dead. In many ways, Bebb is a life giver like Orpheus: he has raised Brownie from the dead, he allegedly renews Herman Redpath's sexual prowess through prayer, and he sustains everyone he meets. Like Orpheus, he seeks to rescue the dying from Hades.

Looking out the train window at the bleak November sky as he travels through New Jersey, Parr feels disconnected from everyone, including his dying sister. As he sees the gray sky,

> I felt like Dante being ferried across into limbo with the spirits of the doomed fluttering about him *comme d'autunno si levan le foglie*, as he says—those autumn leaves again. (23)

In "The Inferno," part one of *The Divine Comedy*, Dante enters the underworld and is ferried across the river Styx (the river of forgetfulness) where he visits the lost souls in Hades. The autumn imagery, the sense of death, forgetfulness, and purposelessness, is reinforced by the mythological and literary references. Archetypal imagery, emphasized in Jungian psychology, reflects the spiritual dimensions of life, which in reference to Dante have a Christian as well as a mythological base. It also signifies the psychological exploration of the unconscious.

Woven into the literary references and given similar archetypal connotations are allusions to opera, an art form Antonio the Italian identifies with. He knows he needs more *"fortissimo"* in his life, sensing the sterility and passiveness of his relationship with Ellie. Various operatic scenes flash through his mind and whenever he is emotionally moved, he pictures the moment as breaking into an aria. The central operatic moment occurs when he is reading from *The Apocryphal New Testament* borrowed from Bebb's library. As he reads the tale of Christ's descent into Hell to rescue Adam and other captive souls (the Harrowing of Hell), Antonio pictures Christ as Mozart's Don Giovanni, the Great Lover with a smile like Errol Flynn, defeating Satan with a single blow. Thus Buechner gives Christ's Harrowing of Hell, which is difficult for moderns to believe, an operatic license as an art form which assumes a willing suspension of disbelief.

Originally titled *The Harrowing*, the novel was renamed *Lion Country* just prior to publication, and indeed the theme of giving life, to the dead and the living dead, characterizes Leo Bebb. Bebb is Orpheus descending to rescue souls from the underworld. Antonio identifies with Dante's descent into Hades, and later vividly pictures Christ's harrowing Hell to set the captives free. As Guy Davenport notes in his review of *Lion Country* in the *New York Times Book Review*,

> When we notice that the novel begins on the subway stairs, with several pointed references to Orpheus . . . , that it has a Harrowing of Hell at its center, that men among lions has a decided Christian ring to it . . . we realize that we are reading a parable. On one level we are being told about the reassessment of goals and values which joggles the elbow of every 40-year-old. On another, we are being reminded that the spirit of Christianity is more a matter of energy and awareness than of forms and rites. (7)

Thus Buechner's approach to psycho-spirituality employs mythological, archetypes drawn from classical opera, myth and epic poetry, to convey the universal truths which are present in psychology and depth spirituality.

When Antonio goes to his dying sister for his last significant visit, she again raises the question of life after death. Whereas previously he brushed off her concerns with a sarcastic Freudian remark, now he relates his Italian operatic rendition of Christ's Harrowing of Hell to which she replies *"Bene, bene,* Antonio." (88). Thus she calls her brother by his adult, Christian name for the first time, indicating an acceptance of his spiritual answer.

Similar to his pervasive recounting of his dreams and myths, Parr's psychological perspective comes through his constant self-analysis. For instance, while he is still "Tono" he analyzes his motives for not telling his sister about his ordination:

> Was it out of some fear that if I told her I had been ordained, even by a charlatan, she would look at me for something more than I felt I had in me to give—my deathbed expertise, the "sweet reprieve and ransom" that Father Hopkins describes having tended to Felix Randall .... Or was it a deep fear still that she would laugh more definitively at the slapstick of it than somehow I quite could myself at that point, which was of course the real slapstick of it? I don't know. (9)

Tono is trying to understand himself and his non-actions. He is analyzing his fears and as a Prufrockian modernist is so inwardly directed that he often cannot act. He is also not able to find a clear answer, because there is none. Later as Antonio he does in fact come up with a "sweet reprieve and ransom" at his sister's deathbed when he pictures for her the Harrowing of Hell. He attributes this to an inspiration beyond himself:

> Three or four times in my life it has been given to me, as Brownie might have put it, to say the

right thing, and this was one of them. I take no credit for it anyway. The Hindu monkey just happened to reach out for the right branch at the right time, that's all, and was lucky enough to catch hold of it. (88)

As W. Dale Brown emphasizes in his introductory overview of Buechner's works, Buechner refuses to discount the problematic side of faith. Thus even in this incidence when Antonio is "given" the right thing, he subverts the miraculous quality by allowing for the "Hindu monkey" of random chance, a concept Parr refers to as an alternative he considers alongside his Freudian self analysis. The term first appears as he is analyzing why he has reacted so violently against Leo Bebb. As Parr watches his cat's agony while coming out of the veterinarian's anesthesia, he associates the suffering animal with his dying sister, then projects blame onto Leo Bebb. He does not know exactly why he does this, but in any case, he is aware that something beyond his own psychological pathology is involved. This open-ended notion of the "Hindu monkey" leaves room for the operation of unconscious drives or divine intervention or blind chance. In his charged emotional state in looking for a paradigm to explain his vehemence in projecting blame onto Bebb, Parr assumes the operatic quality of revenge tragedy and breaks into aria:

> And in my bloodshot and grief-crazed eyes the betrayer, the villain, the one who was somehow responsible for what was happening there on those two sad beds which in my mind had become one, was Bebb. I vowed his destruction. . . .
> Why Bebb? In Hindu iconography, I have read somewhere, the mind of man is portrayed as a monkey swinging from tree to tree, witless, purposeless, grabbing out at whatever new branch happens to come to hand, which I take to mean

> that it is not we who control our thoughts but circumstances that control them. . . And yet, although I doubt I could have explained it at the time, I think there was a kind of crazy logic to it too. We are none of us entirely simian.
>
> If Bebb had been a real priest instead of a phony, he might have been able to help. . . .Help who? Help Miriam and Tom in their dying, or at least help me in my helpless watching? Help how? I don't know how, but if Bebb had been real instead of a phony, he would have known. If there had been any priests anywhere who were real, they might have been able to help. . . making Bebb personally responsible for the failure of the priesthood in general, blaming Bebb personally for the bankruptcy of God. I would probably not have put it that way at the time, but I suspect this was part of what lay behind my shaking fist and bloodshot glance. (18)

As Tono's introspection continues, he comes to realize that ultimately he is blaming Bebb for his own sense of helplessness:

> . . . it had to do, I think, with my being Catholic. . . . [I would occasionally] light a kind of rabbit's-foot candle to Saint Anthony, who, as both my patron saint and the saint who watches over lost things, seemed worthy of my special attention. . . . [I still] had this notion that once a priest always a priest, that however far Bebb had fallen, he still bore the mark upon him like an old tatoo or an appendix scar. He *should* have been able to help. He *should* have been real. And if he had been real—the more I think about it, the more I believe this may have been the real nub of it—then I would

also have been real.

...if Bebb had been a real priest, then I whom he had however absurdly ordained would however absurdly have been able to do these things. I would have been a real priest myself. All of which is a roundabout way of saying that I think I blamed Bebb for my own inadequacy. (18-19)

Psychologically, Tono recognizes his projection and displacement of anger onto Bebb, which may have been random "and yet" had a certain logic to it. What he does not realize even later is that in many ways he has become a priest, albeit a very unorthodox one. Three times he hears confession (from his sister, his nephew and his wife). He administers a kind of last rites to his dying sister as he "received the words to say." He takes in his orphaned nephews and in spite of his many failings, lingering questions and doubts, he tries to comfort the needy, Lucille and Brownie.

Although themes of doubt, ambivalence, psychological uncertainty are certainly present, in the Bebb novels there is a change in tone that tips the balance toward faith. In previous novels, the central character was grappling with emerging faith and just beginning to see the mystery of a transcendent power. Although Leo Bebb makes mistakes, has difficult times, and in *Love Feast* almost looses his sense of mission, he listens to his life through his faith. When questioned by Antonio about what he believes, Bebb responds "I believe everything," but "It's hard as Hell." (BB 143) When asked by his daughter Sharon about his faith Bebb admits that "When the time of testing comes, I'll just have to say, Savior, let thy grace be sufficient. Jesus, take pity on this wore-out tail of mine that's all I got left to bet with" (BB 390).

As Parr's alter ego, Bebb listens to his life through the screen of Scripture. Faith in the reality of God's providence and trust in biblical truth are part and parcel of his Southern fundamentalism, so Bebb's language mixes provincial grammatical errors with rolling phrases from the King James Bible. Contrasting with Bebb's unswerving religious conviction, the narrator Antonio Parr approaches Bebb and the faith he personifies through Freudian analysis and skepticism. Yet through Parr's observations we notice a growing appreciation for Bebb. "Bebbsian" enthusiasm and faith bring life and hope. Despite his foolishness, Bebb is a "life giver," Buechner's equivalent of a saint. Remembering Bebb, Parr asks himself,

> what was there about him that made me miss him more than any man?
> Even at his lowest and bluest, there was a life in him that rubbed off on you, that's all. You might feel better or you might feel worse when Bebb was around, but in any case you felt more. There was more of you to feel with. (BB 434)

According to Freud, the most basic conflict in an individual's psyche was between *Eros* (Love) and *Thanatos* (Death). Buechner's characters may be seen in terms of their connection to the love/life force or the death force, or their movement between the two. Decathexis, an emotional detachment from life, is the psychological condition that continually threatens to overcome Parr. He suffers from a deep sense of alienation (identifying with Dante's descent to visit the dead) as he begins his journey in *Lion Country*. When he is estranged from his wife and son, seeking to fill his emptiness with a sexual encounter, he describes his state of decathexis, a separation from life experienced by elderly persons approaching death.

The major antidote for the death force in Parr's experience is the influence of Leo Bebb, because he is a life-giver whose spiritual life is contagious. Many scholars have noted the change which takes place in Parr's character. According to Stacy Thompson, Antonio is "working his way back from withdrawal to the kind of engagement and transformation" he experienced at the end of *Lion*

Country" (141). Margaret Wimsatt notes Antonio Parr has become wiser and kinder. Brown points out that "like Lear, who, according to one of Tono's students, undergoes a transformation in the direction of kindness (BB 177), Antonio learns to look at the world with, if not new, at least changed eyes" (Brown diss. 248). Yet Brown is quick to add "Tono, like Peter Cowley, Theodore Nicolet, and Tip Ringkoping [protagonists in Buechner's earlier novels], is best characterized by his sense of incompleteness, his longing" (249).

Antonio's incompleteness and longing are not entirely negative, for they reflect a gnawing yearning for the mysterious, loving providence in the *Book of Bebb*. In the book's introduction, Buechner explains he wrote the novels as "a kind of love letter."

> Apart from who the characters are and the places they go and the things they do, there is the sense of what the old hymn quaveringly addresses as "O love that will not let me go," the sense of an ultimate depth to things that is not finally indifferent as to whether people sink or swim but endlessly if always hiddenly refuses to abandon them ... Maybe the reason any book about something like real life is a love-letter is that in the last analysis that is what real life is too. (BB ix)

This sense of God's providence working out in the past, present, and future is what Antonio Parr is beginning to glimpse at the end of *Lion Country*. Through self-exposure, confession, and acceptance of the past, he realizes that becoming a life giver like Leo Bebb involves courageously facing the truth about yourself and about life, and moving on. In his retrospective self-appraisal he states:

> All of which goes to show, as if that were necessary, that you cannot escape the past or the

future either, and at my best and bravest I do not even want to escape them. Miriam's death, the faceless baby, Lucille's Tropicanas and in a way also Brownie's smile and that slightly mad and rebellious eye of Bebb's—all the sad and hurtful things of the past I would prevent having happened if I could, but, failing that, I would not wish the hurt of them away even if that were possible.

....And at my best and bravest I do not want to escape the future either, even though I know that it contains what will someday be my own great and final pain. Because a distaste for dying is twin to a taste for living, and again I don't think you can tamper with one without somehow doing mischief to the other. (BB 128)

Later, on a more somber note, the reality of life's ironies, the sense that his marriage is imperfect, is part of his maturing. In his self assessment at the end of *Love Feast*, Antonio has found "a capacity if not for rising above irony like the saints, at least for living it out with something like grace, with the suspicion if not the certainty that maybe the dark and hurtful shadows all things cast are only shadows" (404).

Antonio Parr's Lone Ranger dreams recorded in *Love Feast* and *Treasure Hunt* symbolize his groping faith and sense of something that will not abandon him. With the sound track of the William Tell Overture theme for the 1950s television Western playing in the background, the mysterious masked man riding the white horse always comes through, leaving behind the faint sound of his presence in the failing light. As Antonio dreams of the Lone Ranger and his faithful sidekick Tonto, he hears the words "Kemo Sabe," faithful friend, a reminder of the "love that will not let me go." Like the Indian sidekick, Tonto, the Tono side of his heart can't help but whisper "Kemo Sabe" to the one who just may be there. In the *Love Feast* dream Antonio is given a new name.

This name is secret but like the new name given each believer in the Book of Revelation, it holds the key to his real identity. In the *Treasure Hunt* dream, under the influence of Babe's light ray or hypnosis, as the Lone Ranger comes to the rescue in the knick of time on his white horse, he metaphorically represents the second coming of Christ in the Book of Revelation to bring justice and mercy to those who await his coming. As he takes off his mask, Antonio is almost blinded by the blazing light of his face.

Treasure Hunt, the last novel in the *Book of Bebb*, ends with Antonio Parr the English teacher quoting Shakespeare as he concludes the account of his own search for "whatever it is that is always missing." As Antonio listens to his life, he hears "Time's winged chariot hurrying near," knowing he is getting older and his time is limited. But at the same time he hears "the Tonto afoot in the dusk of me somewhere who, not because he ought to but because he can't help himself, whispers Kemo Sabe every once in a while to what may or may not be only a silvery trick of the failing light" (530).

As the opening quote from Buechner's memoir *Now and Then* suggests, Buechner believes that truth about ourselves is revealed in dreams where the unconscious is manifested freely, a process similar to what sometimes happens in writing fiction. Freud might say the subconscious conflict of Eros and Thanatos is allowed to surface. In his writing the *Book of Bebb*, the spiritual and the psychological sides of Buechner find outward expression as individual characters. As object relations theory would describe it, Tono is the doubter while Bebb represents the believer, the life giver. Tono hangs back, ready to qualify his faith with Freudian analysis, while Bebb is open and willing to risk being exposed.

Both characters contain a side of the author, who looks back over his life and glimpses the hand of providence guiding him along his "sacred journey." Perhaps like the skeptical Antonio Parr, this revelation of presence is only seen "now and then" to borrow the words of Tillich and the title of Buechner's second memoir. But that is the point. Bebbsian faith and Tonian doubt often co-exist in one person. In *The Book of Bebb* the two are embodied as individual psyches and take on lives of their own. In the next two novels to be discussed, the psychological and spiritual are unified in the protagonist as Godric and Jacob each learn to listen in their lives to the love that will not let them go.

Notes

1 In "Sanctifying the Profane," one of the first dissertations on Buechner's fiction written in 1976, Nancy Beth Myers discussed religious themes in Buechner's novels.

2 Freud took the word "psyche" for the human soul, spirit, or mind, from the Greek myth of Psyche, who descended into the underworld to prove her love for Cupid. Only after a harrowing journey, where she performed arduous tasks for Venus, could she be reunited with him. Thus psychoanalysis deals with investigating the underlying unconscious mental processes to work through repressed conflicts which block the individual's emotional well-being.

5

Godric: A Medieval Saint Remembers

We cannot undo our old mistakes or their consequences any more than we can erase old wounds that we have both suffered and inflicted, but through the power that memory gives us of thinking, feeling, imagining our way back through time we can at long last finally finish with the past in the sense of removing the power to hurt us and other people and to stunt our growth as human beings.... It is through memory that we are able to reclaim much of our lives that we have long since written off by finding that in everything that has happened to us over the years God was offering us possibilities of new life and healing which, though we may have missed them at the time, we can still choose and be brought to life by and healed by all these years later.

Another way of saying it, perhaps, is that memory makes it possible for us both to bless the past, even those parts of it that we have always felt cursed by, and also to be blessed by it. If this kind of remembering sounds like what psychotherapy is all about, it is because of course it is, but I think it is also what the forgiveness of sins is all about—the interplay of God's forgiveness of us and our forgiveness of God and each other. (TS 32-33)

In *Godric* (1980) Frederick Buechner's psychological spirituality finds its ultimate literary expression as an old monk listens to his life. The fictionalized memoir of an actual twelfth-century saint, Buechner's tenth novel embodies his use of psychotherapeutic dynamics to convey spiritual truths. Psychotherapy takes place in an unlikely venue: the hermit's cell where an old holy man is approaching death. The scribe Reginald, like a prodding therapist, queries Godric about his past, causing him to remember and reexperience his long, adventurous life. Through Godric's interior monologue, the reader is privy to the saint's autobiographical confession, reading both his oral and his mental responses to the scribe who seeks to write his sanctified hagiography. This plausible encounter of monk and scribe takes on a psychological framework that Buechner uses to expose the inner workings of his protagonist's heart and soul. The random thought associations formed as Godric remembers the past and the spontaneity of intuitive connections arising out of his process of self-discovery resemble Buechner's own autobiographical journal, *Alphabet of Grace*. In *Godric* the reader overhears the old saint listening to his life. As he remembers, confesses, and repents, he discovers a new understanding of forgiveness and grace.

Godric is far more than the self-discovery prompted by a psychotherapy session, however, for the entire structure of the novel reflects the flow of Godric's memory of past and present. He tells his story from "both ends at once" (165), beginning with his youth and remembering backwards from the present until "at last both Godrics meet—the one who was, together with the one who is . . . . The third's the Godric yet to be . . . " (165). In poetic language, he remembers being marooned on a roof above the raging floodwaters of the River Wear. Experiencing his memory like the raging waves of the wild river, he wonders, " is the past a sea old men can founder in before their time and drown?" Like the rising and falling of waves, the past and present ebb and flow through Godric's mind as he relates the events of his life not in chronological order, but in overlapping and intersecting layers of his memory.

Like the structure of the narrative and the novel's theme, the flow of present realities and past memories, surface appearance and inner pain, are reflected in the imagery of the novel. The real hurt self beneath the false self is described in metaphors of foul and fair. Underlying reality exposed beneath surface appearance is thus reflected in Godric's memory and the novel's figurative language. The psychotherapeutic need to reexperience the past hurt trail to find inner healing (the love story) is the essence of Godric's spiritual and psychological journey. In keeping with the novel's setting, in place of the psychoanalytic language characteristic of Antonio Parr, narrator of *The Book of Bebb*, psychological principles are formulated in terms of medieval spirituality and its metaphorical imagery of self-denial. Of particular interest is the imagery of starvation and the contrast of spiritual and physical hunger and satisfaction which is central to the narrative itself and has special significance in light of Buechner's own experience while writing the novel. Thus, while containing an astute psychological and spiritual analysis, the literary quality of *Godric* stands on its own, as its critical reception and nomination for the Pulitzer Prize make clear. Understanding the ways Buechner uses psychological dynamics in this novel only adds to our appreciation of its literary excellence.

Inversions of chronology, paradoxical treatment of friendship and hagiography, and psychological dynamics which in subtle ways reflect Buechner's life as author and Christian, are embodied in the novel's structure, theme, characterization, voice, and imagery to create a unified, organic, and high-quality work of literature.

Inversion of chronology is the major structural device, which in *Godric* flows naturally out of the narrative technique. Through interior dialogue, which provides access to the thoughts as well as the words of the narrator, present thoughts and past memories continually interact to dynamically portray the old man engaged in listening to his life. Much of the subject matter, told in the first person, is reminiscent of St. Augustine's *Confessions*, as the medieval monastic talks about his spiritual journey, confessing his sins, regrets, and failures but also recalling unexpected and undeserved times of spiritual visitation and transformation. Godric is, however, far more profane than Augustine, and the details of his life as well as the coarseness of his language leave no doubt that a roughshod beast is still slouching in his mind. Traditional hagiography, which portrays the exemplary life of the saint, is thus subverted by the rude language of the subject (as opposed to the baroque language of the scribe who reads sections of the official hagiography in the last chapter), his anti-clerical remarks, and his self-depreciation. At the same time, in Godric's own mind, spiritual visitations, miracles, and demonic battles are included as factual occurrences or qualified with "I think." Visions are accompanied by admission of surprise and shame because he feels unworthy of them.

In *The Book of Bebb*, Buechner also used a self-deprecating narrator, but Antonio Parr was an outsider, a non-believing skeptic who warily examined the religious protagonist, thinking he was probably a con man. Chronologically, the narration was straightforward and although Parr's attitude underwent changes and became more open to the spiritual, his interior identity and introspection about his past were not as important as his changing view of the protagonist. However, in *Godric*, the narrator is the "holy man" himself, an old man, nearing death.

Godric's interaction with Reginald also provides comic relief for an otherwise serious confession. Through stream of consciousness, the memories flow back and forth (like the ever present River Wear) between his present interaction in telling his story to Reginald, the scribe, and his past memories of the events as he recalls them. While admitting to himself his inner conflicts, his regrets, and his failures, Godric continuously berates the scribe for trying to write the hagiography he feels he does not deserve. As Reginald provides "spiritual" interpretations, Godric rudely contradicts him, sometimes aloud and sometimes in his mind. Thus there is a running dialogue within the protagonist's mind and between the two main characters, stimulating Godric to recount his past in response to Reginald's questions and simultaneously providing holy and unholy interpretations of the account. Thus the fair/foul theme is conveyed through the inverted chronology as well as the often comic collision of the two characters. Psychologically, Buechner is using humor and off-color references to make a spiritual confession entertaining and realistic.

Buechner's clever use of language and humor is particularly effective to subvert the hagiography while showing the self-deprecating and unsentimental quality of Godric's character. Psychotherapy, to be effective, breaks through ego defenses (the false self) to expose the real self within, a principle to which Godric is committed. For example, when the two men discuss the etymology of Godric's name, the cross purposes of the linguistic debate between Reginald, the hagiographer, and Godric, the devil's advocate, are vividly portrayed:

> "Aedwen named you well, Father," says Reginald in his coddling lilt.
> I say, "Father, my bum."
> "A holy name for a babe born to be holy," he says.
> "Fiddle my faddle," I say or nothing at all in words but something instead in the fingertalk he doesn't know. He's better off not knowing, if he

only knew.

"The *god* means *God*. That's plain as your nose, I mean no slight. The *ric* is Saxon *reign*. So *God* and *ric* in sum means God reigns, Godric. It means God reigns in you. It means when God comes down at last to weigh the souls of men, he'll not find Godric's wanting, Father Godric."

"Fetch me a bowl to puke in," I tell him. He's got him such a honeyed way I'm ever out to sour it.

"Godric will have his little jest," says Reginald.

So then I teach him other ways to read my name. "*God's god* for sure. You hit that square. But *ric* is Erse for *wreck*," I say, not knowing Erse from arse. "God's wreck I be, it means. God's wrecked Godric for his sins. Or Godric's sins have made a wreck of God."

Reginald throws up his hands, his palms as pale and soft as cheese.

"There's other ways as well," I say. "Rip Godric up another seam, and what you get is *go* and *drick*."

"What's *drick*?" says Reginald.

"A foul Welsh word not fit for monkish ears," I say.

"How great is your *humilitas*, Father," Reginald says.

I say, "Yet, Mother, not so great as is my drick." (17-18)

To portray the psychotherapeutic aspect of remembering the past and the confession of sin, Buechner uses time as a structural device through inversions of chronology (flashback within flashbacks, mingling of past and present events and dialogue within the mind of the old saint), as theme (memory as a key to psychological and spiritual understanding), and in figurative language. In this confessional memoir, the flow of time is a reflection of larger philosophical truth, the relationship of past, present and future, which still bothers Godric as an old man. Though troubled by the future he foresees supernaturally, he is more tormented by memories of his past. He confides in the Abbot Ailred:

> "But oh, the times that were, they're worse. . . . For now I'm long past mending them. Yet still they flood their banks like Wear and roar at me. Oh Ailred, is the past a sea old men can founder in before their time and drown?" (58).

Watching the storm-tossed Wear atop the little chapel, the wise abbot Ailred tells Godric:

> "You speak of time, Godric. . . . Time is a storm. Times past and times to come, they heave and flow and leap their bounds like Wear. Hours are clouds that change their shapes before your eyes . . . . But beyond time's storm and clouds there's timelessness. Godric, the Lord of Heaven changes not, and even when our view's most dark, he's there above us fair and golden as the sun." And so it is.
> "God's never gone," my gentle, ailing Ailred said. "It's only men go blind." (60-61)

Psychotherapy, the remembering of the past in order to heal and bless it and the forgiveness of sins is seen in the outworking of Godric's self-reflective narrative. The reexperiencing of past painful memories plagues Godric as he reviews his life, and his biggest regret is that he cannot "mend" the past. By the end of the novel, having struggled through the storm of his past, he emerges with memories also of the healing touches and transcendent visitations he experienced along the way. Thus memory has been both painful and redemptive. After the review of his life, Godric is able to see the past in the larger perspective, to which Ailred referred, and even internally to ask Reginald's forgiveness and to bless the hagiography, although he still refuses to be called a saint.

Although critics did not do a psychological analysis of why this novel was so effective, they were impressed by the depth of character, which combined ambivalence and honest spirituality and Buechner's creative language. Writing a lengthy review for the *Times Literary Supplement*, Peter Lewis praised the novel's literary qualities calling it a "stylistic tour de force," an engaging "picaresque narrative" and "an ideal means of exploring the nature of spirituality" (278). In the *Atlantic Monthly* P. L. Adams extolled it as a "remarkable work" and a "true work of art" (96). In contrast to their review of *The Final Beast*, *Newsweek* also praised it highly:

> Like all good writers of historical fiction, Buechner strives less for verisimilitude than for a vision of the past.... In telling his long story in such a short space, and from both of its ends at once, Buechner glides deftly from the fanciful to scenes that are nearly realistic.... I think Buechner has risked much in attempting to define the ambivalence in the life of a saintly man, and risked even more by adopting a language that could easily have become overwrought. In a year in which most American novels have seemed either tedious or flaccid enterprises, *Godric* glimmers brightly. (Prescott 114)

In contrast to the reaction to *The Final Beast*, the critics appreciated Buechner's handling of "the nature of spirituality," and "the ambivalence of the life of a saintly man." Likewise, the reviewer for the Jesuit publication *America* extolled Godric's "unmistakable evidence of fiction's power as a medium of religious meaning.... [Buechner] fashioned a narrative voice for a novel about a holy man that is both thoroughly human and yet deeply moving" (May 348). What struck both secular and religious critics were the novel's stylistic literary qualities and its deft depiction of the sinner/saint ambivalence in the central character. Writing in the *Times Literary Supplement,* Lewis stated,

> In the extraordinary figure of Godric, both stubborn outsider and true child of God, both worldly and unworldly, Buechner has found an ideal means of exploring the nature of spirituality. ...Buechner transforms Reginald's [hagiographic] account by re-creating Godric as a complex, full bodied character who tells his own story in a decidedly undevotional way....Yet the difficult old cuss . . . emerges—almost in spite of his account of himself—as a true holy man with a great love of God's entire creation. (278)

Of Buechner's ten earliest novels, only *Godric* is still in print. Considered by many his best novel, it is also Buechner's personal favorite. In *The Final Beast* Buechner tried to portray a similar ambivalent man of God, but some critics felt it was unconvincing. In *Godric* the use of first-person narration and a natural presentation of the inner dynamics of psychotherapy and spirituality produced a work both secular and religious readers found remarkable.

Yet Buechner is still relatively unknown in the academy, perhaps because he does not fit into accepted categories of American literature. Writers with a spiritual orientation such as Flannery O'Connor and Walker Percy are often read in the context of Southern literature. Though often compared to John Updike in his modernism, he is very different philosophically, especially in the area of spirituality. To date, published scholarship on his work has been written by those who share Buechner's beliefs and therefore tend to valorize his spiritual concerns. This becomes problematic for, as Bruinooge and Engbers argue in "Frederick Buechner's *Godric*: Sinner and Saint recomplicated,"

> a good amount of this [limited scholarship] is appreciative and reductive rather than critical. The problem arises from the dynamic of a Christian author read most often by Christian critics, who may be looking for a validation of their belief or for a mimetic reinforcement of Buechner's theological ideas in his nonfiction. Marie-Helene Davies represents this tendency in *Laughter in a Genevan Gown*. She reads *Godric* as "The story of the gradual conversion of a pirate into a holy hermit" (66). Her reading, as well as perceiving Godric's life as a simple progression from godlessness to grace, posits a progression parallel to that of Buechner himself as author and Christian. Such a reading, however, minimizes the subtleties of the work and ignores the background of its author in literary modernism. *Godric* resists a simplistic interpretation through inversions of chronology and a deep and often paradoxical treatment of issues of friendship and hagiography. Ultimately, Buechner's subtleties serve the novel better both as a work of high quality contemporary literature and as a Christian voice. (35)

The inversions of chronology and paradoxical treatment of friendship and hagiography which Bruinooge and Engbers stress emerge from the interplay of psychological and spiritual dynamics that makes *Godric* so convincing. In his sacrilegious honesty, Godric breaks through psychological and spiritual defenses to the reveal the wounded inner self. Buechner is able to do this convincingly because from his own experience he knows the importance of memory as a way to both remember and bless the past, an experience he relates to psychotherapy and the forgiveness of sins (TS 32-33).

Like the vacillating quality of time and memory, Godric's progression from scoundrel to saint is not neatly linear, an essential aspect in the portrayal of psychological and spiritual dynamics of human beings. As Bruinooge and Engbers demonstrate, saintly elements in the young Godric, as well as spiritual visitation, mingle with carnal elements in the aged saint, creating a complex and rounded protagonist. Although more fully developed, Godric is another in a long line of Buechner protagonists, heroes standing "ankle deep in mud." "Scratch fair, find foul" (114), the paranoid hermit Elric tells Godric, echoing the witches' prophecy in Shakespeare's *Macbeth*. This fair/foul duality is a major theme in Buechner's modernist vision. Elric's negative assessment is not the end of the story, however, but the beginning.

The fair/foul theme is metaphorically represented throughout the novel. In one vivid instance, Godric recounts his service as steward for Falkes de Granvill, whom Reginald admires as "a noble lord." De Granvill's underlying wickedness is physically portrayed by the foul dining room floor lying beneath a fair covering. As his wife Hedwic tells Godric,

> "My lord this morning bade me tell the chamberlain to have them sweeten it with herbs against the feast, and so I did. They scattered lavender and mint and winter savory all about till now it's fit for royal feet . . . . . I doubt if there's a sweeter floor in all of Christendom. But, Godric, do you know what's underneath?" . . . .
>
> "What's underneath is turds of dogs and grease and spit and bits of bone," she said. "The part you see if fair and fresh. The part you do not see is foul. Do you know what it reminds me of,

this floor?"
Again I shook my head though I had guessed her meaning well enough.
"My life," she said, and hid her face. (84-85)

Awareness of fair/foul duality is painful yet intrinsic to Godric's understanding of life and of himself. According to Allen's terminology to describe the psychodynamics of emotional healing, one must experience one's hurt trail to gain insight into painful memories as a prerequisite to discovering one's love story. This is what Godric's therapeutic self-analysis of his life as an old man allows him to do. Reginald is seeking to sugarcoat the past, to present a sanitized hagiography. In contrast, Godric admits his wrongdoing and mixed motives to reveal the foul beneath the supposed fair.

What makes Godric different from the modernist anti-hero is that alongside his "foul" self, he discovers the presence of God. When he is least deserving, he realizes he has received visitations from Christ and saintly intercessors. In his youth, when he almost drowned, he heard Christ's voice. Although he ignored the offer to "hold fast to him who gave his life for thee and thine" (15), he knew Christ was calling him. While still living in the world, he received visitations from John the Baptist, the Virgin Mary, St. Cuthbert and the angel Gillian. As an old man remembering these times, Godric's sorrowful acknowledgement of his unworthiness only underscores God's faithfulness. Like Thompson's Hound of Heaven, God will not abandon Godric, and as he remembers times of past visitations, he is filled with gratitude.

Figurative language, subversion of hagiography, and ambivalence of friendship (as Bruinooge and Engbers note) reflect the duality and paradox of fair/foul imagery that run through *Godric*. The modernist anti-hero full of angst and alienation is one side of the strange old hermit. Yet, a genuine spiritual quality is also present, seen frequently throughout the novel as Godric spontaneously speaks directly to God in prayer, admitting failure, asking forgiveness, and praying for those around him. Awareness of his faults causes him to maintain a confessional dialogue with God as he expresses his innermost longings. God is as much a part of his consciousness as his memories and his interactions with Reginald. This spiritual relationship is not expressed in abstract philosophical terms. When speaking of God, the imagery is taken from the natural world. The metaphorical quality of Godric's imagery of darkness and light, storm and sun, river and sea, and even hungering and thirsting, gives abstract concepts a concrete quality, drawing spiritual truths from personal experience and nature like the parables of Christ. Because St. Godric was also the first lyric poet in English, the vivid quality of his metaphorical language is consistent with his character and adds a natural poetic quality to his speech.

Within the medieval world of saints, angels and demons, the historical Godric comes alive as Buechner allows his own psychological and spiritual struggles to shape his protagonist. According to literary scholar Frederick Crews, "An author's psychology takes coloration from every element in his background, genetic endowment, upbringing, and milieu, and it leaves its signature not just on plots and images but on everything he does" (12). Certainly Buechner's signature is on *Godric*.

What were the circumstances which united within the author to shape this unique literary work? When asked by a journalist how he came to write *Godric*, Buechner replied,

> I . . . picked up the little *Penguin Dictionary of Saints*. . . opened it up just by accident to Godric, whom I'd never heard of. I was just enchanted by him. And then it suddenly occurred to me that this was Bebb in an earlier incarnation. Of all my books, it's the one I like best, and it was something I didn't have to struggle for. It was on the house. (Nelson 44)

This novel was "on the house" and one Buechner "didn't have to struggle for" yet he admitted it came out of one of the darkest periods of his life. During the writing of *Godric,* Buechner's struggle was not in the creative process but in his personal life and his concern for his daughter. Buechner described writing the novel as a kind of therapy which allowed him to "keep his sanity." For Buechner, its composition, like psychotherapy, involved working through painful experiences to gain insights and find connections that brought resolution and healing.

Yeats has observed that from the struggle with the world we make rhetoric; from the struggle with ourselves we create art. This is true for the novel *Godric* which so convincingly portrays the protagonist's struggle and, when seen in light of what Frederick Buechner was experiencing at the time, the author's inner conflicts as well. In the psychological and spiritual dimensions of Buechner's work, *Godric* is the most telling example of the artist's unconscious conflicts producing art.

This said, the novel is far more than a romantic expression of the author's repressed angst. And yet, in his memoirs Buechner portrays the writing of his books as events situated within his personal experience. Although his novels should not be reduced to biographical or psychological studies of the author's conflicts, additional insights can be gained by investigating Buechner's statements about his experience in writing *Godric:*

> And all the time those things [his daughter's near fatal eating disorder and his subsequent feelings of fear and helplessness] were happening, the very fact that I was able to save my sanity by continuing to write among other things a novel called *Godric* made my work blessed and a means of grace at least for me. Nothing I've ever written came out of a darker time or brought me more light and comfort. It also—far more than I realized at the time I wrote it—brought me a

> sharper glimpse than I had ever had before of the crucial role my father has always played in my life and continues to play in my life even though in so many ways I have long since lost all but a handful of conscious memories of him. (TS 20-21)

Within the context of the interplay of psychology and spirituality, Buechner associated writing *Godric* with "saving my sanity." At the time of composition, he was undergoing powerful emotion which may or may not have been "repressed" in terms of his awareness of feeling the loss of his father and his subsequent codependency and fusion with his daughter. Certainly at the time, Buechner was struggling with the unbearable pain of almost losing her. So it is that the ambivalence of familial love and friendship is a central theme in the novel, and in the first chapter, Godric poignantly asks, "What's friendship, when all's done, but the giving and taking of wounds?" (7). This painful recognition leads the aged Godric to pray, "Gentle Jesu, Mary's son, be thine the wounds that heal our wounding. Press thy bloody scars to ours that thy dear blood may flow in us and cleanse our sin" (7-8). Responding to the emotional pain of his hurt trail, Godric seeks transference to the wounds of Christ for healing of memories and forgiveness of sin. Christ is the wounded healer, a picture of what Godric is also becoming.

In *Now and Then,* Buechner states that he realized his own unconscious identification with Godric's relationship with his father, Aedlward, after he had completed the book. Godric's father is a relatively minor character in the novel, however.

Far more central to the novel than Godric's father is his sister Burcwen, but Buechner hardly mentions this character in his memoirs. For Burcwen, Godric is a father figure as well as a brother (she is much younger and looks up to Godric). The central wounding of the narrative that causes Godric the most pain is his excessive love for Burcwen, a love that in the novel culminates in incest. Her codependency and fusion with Godric and the severe anorexia that she develops in response to their incestuous relationship parallels Buechner's own struggles with his daughter at the time he wrote the book. This is not to suggest that the novel "reveals" that Buechner committed incest with his daughter. Far more probable is the author's subconscious metaphorical instinct which translated an emotional fusion into its most dramatic expression.

To base literary readings solely on psychological insights can be reductionist, using literature to validate a particular theory (as Freud did with *Hamlet* to demonstrate the Oedipus Complex). Critical scholar Frederick Crews explains how his psychoanalytic reading of Hawthorne in The *Sins of the Fathers: Hawthorne's Psychological Themes* (1966) suffered from overzealous methodizing.[1] The New Critics warned against the "intentional fallacy,"[2] the error of interpreting literature in terms of the author's supposed intention, whether conscious or unconscious, rather than what was "objectively" in the work.[3]

Nevertheless, it is evident that the unconscious, which Buechner calls the place where dreams come from, is involved in the creative process.[4] Buechner's statements show he was not aware of his own unconscious issues in the novel until long after it was published. In a 1981 interview for the evangelical journal *Christianity Today*, Buechner discussed his most recent novel, *Godric*, published just the year before. Buechner was asked about his use of autobiographical material in his fiction:

> In *The Alphabet of Grace* you say that at its heart most theology, like most fiction, is essentially autobiography. How autobiographical is your work?
>
> [Buechner]: By and large, I haven't drawn very heavily on my own life in my novels—except my fantasy life. There are certain exceptions, of course. In *The Final Beast* the conversion experiences of the minister Nicolet were very

much my own. And Kuykendall, the clergyman-professor in *The Return of Ansel Gibbs* was modeled on a Union Seminary professor who had a tremendous influence on my life in every way. (Nelson 44)

In this interview, Buechner mentions only a few specific references to situations in his own life which appear in his novels. Although he discussed how he came to pick *Godric* as a subject, in the interview he made no mention of any connections with his own life.

In his memoir *Now and Then* (1983), written after he had been in therapy, Buechner hinted at the personal circumstances surrounding *Godric*. He cryptically referred to the "new leg of the journey that the last novel I wrote is about" by stating,

> We are to love one another as God has loved us. That is the truth of it. But to love one another more than God has loved us—to love one another at the expense of our own freedom to be something like whole and at peace within ourselves, and at the expense of others' freedom, too—is the dark shadow that the truth casts. This is what I started to learn when Katherine and Dinah [Buechner's two oldest daughters] went away to school in 1975 and launched on lives of their own.
>
> It is this new leg of the journey that the last novel [*Godric*] I wrote is about, I suppose, although I don't believe I thought of it that way at the time. (NT 105)

Almost eight years later, writing his third and most self-revealing, psychologically-oriented memoir *Telling Secrets*, Buechner stated that *Godric* brought him "a sharper glimpse than I had ever had before of the crucial role my father has always played in my life and continues to play in my life" (21). Describing the novel as written during one of the darkest periods of his life, he linked his dedication of the book to the memory of his father with his identification with Godric's grief "for having lost a father I never knew." Of particular interest are these comments in *Telling Secrets,* where he shared for the first time the anguish he was experiencing while writing *Godric* and the workings of the unconscious:

> I did not realize until after I wrote it how much of this [the crucial role my father has always played in my life and continues to play in my life] there is in the book. When Godric is about to leave home to make his way in the world and his father Aedlward raises his hand to him in farewell, Godric says, "I believe my way went from that hand as a path goes from a door, and though many a mile that way has led me since, with many a turn and crossroad in between, if ever I should trace it back, it's to my father's hand that it would lead." And later, when he learns of his father's death, he says, "The sadness was I'd lost a father I had never fully found. It's like a tune that ends before you've heard it out. Your whole life through you search to catch the strain, and seek the face you've lost in strangers' faces." In writing passages like that, I was writing more than I had known I knew with the result that the book was not only a word *from* me—my words painstakingly chosen and arranged into sentences by me alone—but also a word out of such a deep and secret part of who I am that it seemed also a word *to* me.
>
> A book you write out of the depths of who you are, like a dream you dream out of those same depths, is entirely your own creation. All

> the words your characters speak are words that you alone have put into their mouths, just as every situation they become involved in is one that you along have concocted for them. But it seems to me nonetheless that a book you write, like a dream you dream, can have more healing and truth and wisdom in it at least for yourself than you feel in any way responsible for.
>
> A large part of the truth that *Godric* had for me was the truth that although death ended my father, it has never ended my relationship with my father—a secret that I had never so clearly understood before. So forty-four years after the last time I saw him, it was to my father that I dedicated the book—*In memoriam patris mei*. I wrote the dedication in Latin solely because at the time it seemed appropriate to the medieval nature of the tale, but I have come to suspect since that Latin was also my unconscious way of remaining obedient to the ancient family law that the secret of my father must be at all costs kept secret. (TS 21-22)

That Buechner was drawing on his own relationship with his father in writing *Godric* is even more apparent in light of how little is actually known about St. Godric's parentage. The historical note included at the end of the novel states Godric was born of Anglo-Saxon parents in 1065, and tells us only that the name of his father was Aedlward. Seemingly extraneously, Buechner creates a sense of paternal abandonment in his protagonist like his own sense of abandonment when his father committed suicide when he was ten.

In his previous books, Buechner's references to this loss are disguised, and only in his memoir *Sacred Journey* (1982) published two years after *Godric* and after he has been in therapy does he describe his father's suicide for the first time. Suicide is ever present in his early novels, however. In *A Long Day's Dying* Tristram Bone's alter ego, the pet monkey, slits his throat by imitating his master's mock suicide. *The Seasons' Difference* has a character who has recently lost her husband who committed suicide. *The Return of Ansel Gibbs* centers around the protagonist's relationship with the son of Rudy Tripp, who committed suicide and closely resembled Buechner's father. In *The Entrance to Porlock*, the suicide of a prep school student causes the cowardly headmaster to face himself and his own mortality. In *The Book of Bebb*, Bebb's wife Lucille commits suicide. Certainly the unconscious effects of his father's suicide underlie much of Buechner's fiction.

In the earlier chapters of *Godric,* the protagonist's personal losses and past failures threaten to overwhelm him as he looks back over his long life. Remembering his youth, Godric has little good to say about his father, Aedlward. In recounting his life story, Godric makes clear his disapproval of Reginald's rose-colored interpretation that his name Aedlward means "Keeper of Blessedness" by responding, "If so, he kept it mostly to himself" (9). Godric only remembers his father's back and the sense of abandonment:

> It seems that he was ever striding off in every way but ours so I scarcely had the time to mark the smile or scowl of him. Even the look of his eyes is gone. They were grey as the sea like mine, it's said, only full of kindness, but what matter how kind a man's eye be if he never fixes you with it long enough to learn? (9)

Reminded of his childhood for Reginald's account, Godric describes his father as faceless, like the wind, and their relationship in terms of hunger and starvation: "It was fear kept Aedlward from us, and next to God what he feared of all things most was an empty belly . . . . So it was his fear we'd starve that made him starve us for that one of all things that we hungered for the most, which was the man himself" (10). Godric recounts having gone to Rome to pray for his father's soul at his mother's request, but feels it is to no avail. On the way home, an angelic presence named Gillian tells Godric she has seen his father in purgatory, shivering with cold, trying to climb a ladder which represents Godric's prayers. As Godric realizes the reality of his father's need and the possible efficacy of his prayers, his attitude changes and he begins to feel compassion for him.

But it is only as he remembers his sojourn in Jerusalem, when he came to understand Christ's suffering and to feel his own burdens and sense of guilt, that he asks forgiveness from Christ and from his father:

> Dear Christ, have mercy on my soul. And Aedlward, have mercy too. I've chided you for failing as a father, too spent from grubbing to have any love to spend on me. Maybe it was the other way around, and it was I that failed you as a son. Did I ever bring you broth? Was any word I ever spoke a word to cheer your weariness? All this, and more than this, I bore upon my back from holy place to holy place. (103)

Psychotherapeutic remembering and healing the past thus come full circle in the forgiveness of sins. In the novel, Godric moves from bitterness at his father's emotional abandonment to understanding and acceptance. Commenting on what he learned from the novel, Buechner recalls, "A large part of the truth that *Godric* had for me was the truth that although death ended my father, it has never ended my relationship with my father" (TS 22). In Buechner's fiction, Godric's prayers to and for his father allow him to be reconciled to him after he is gone. Later in his own psychotherapy, Buechner used a technique recommended by the therapist to get in touch with his own memories and feelings from childhood. Using his left (more childlike and helpless) hand, he wrote out a dialogue with his father, a conversation he wished he could have said to his father, and what his father might have said in return. For Buechner this was a helpful way to say goodbye, giving healthy closure to the relationship which was prematurely severed. Before he had experienced this in therapy, Buechner has Godric experience a similar type of closure in prayer to Christ and his father.

In relating the subconscious conflicts and insights which surfaced through the writing of *Godric,* Buechner emphasizes what it revealed about his relationship with his father. In *Telling Secrets* he stresses the significance of its composition during "a dark time" when his daughter was suffering from a near fatal eating disorder, but other than general references to Godric's learning to let go and accept loss, he does not mention specific connections in the novel to his daughter's anorexia.

A close reading of the novel and later texts reveals many connections, however. In *Whistling in the Dark: A Doubter's Dictionary* (1988), his lexicon of secular words given a spiritual and sometimes humorous twist, published eight years after *Godric,* Buechner includes a definition of "Anorexia":

> Nothing for breakfast. A diet soda for lunch. Maybe a little lettuce.... In time you come to look like a victim of Dachau—the sunken eyes and hollow cheeks, the marionette arms and calfless legs....
>
> Anorexia seems to be a modern disease, but old phrases like "pining away" and "wasting away" suggest it may have been around unnamed for a long time....
>
> .... By starving themselves, anorexics are speaking symbolically, and by trying above all else to make them start eating again, their families are in their own fashion speaking back the same way.

> Far beneath the issue of food there is, on both sides, unspoken issues of love, trust, fear, loss, separation. Father and mother, brother and sister, they are all of them afflicted together, acting out in pantomime a complex, subterranean drama whose nature they are at best only dimly aware of.. And so, one way or another, are we all. . . .
>
> In our sickness, stubbornness, pride, we starve ourselves for what we hunger for above all else. "Speaking the truth in love" is another phrase from Ephesians (4:15). It is the only cure for the anorexia that effects us all. (10)

What becomes evident in a closer reading of *Godric* is the many ways anorexia and Buechner's relationship with his daughter are present in the text, specifically in terms of imagery and theme. The most overt imagery throughout the novel is emaciation, starvation, hunger, skin and bones, wounding and burden bearing. Physical and spiritual hunger are often juxtaposed, as characters seek physical nourishment or physical healing, when their real need is spiritual, though they do not recognize this. As an old man looking back, Godric has ambivalence toward his own powers to heal and the importance of meeting purely physical needs. As an older and wiser man he prays,

> Dear Father, see how these thy children hunger here. They starve for want of what they cannot name. Their poor lost souls are famished. Their foolish hands reach out. Oh grant them richer fare than one old sack of bones whose wits begin to turn. Feed them with something more than Godric here, for Godric's no less starved for thee than they. (122-23)

Yet in the first half of the novel, many of the references to starvation are positively associated with spirituality and dedication to God. In the first chapter, Ailred, the most holy man in the book, comes to pray with Godric and to ask him to allow Reginald to write his life's history. Almost as a sign of his self-denial and dedication to God, Ailred is characterized as emaciated. "He's all bones. Godric's all rags"(6). Pointing out the truth of God's continual presence, he "aimed a bony finger at the sky" (60). Throughout the novel emaciated male bodies are an indication of self-sacrifice for God. Elric, the masochistic ascetic, from whom *Godric* learns the life of a hermit, equates starvation with dedication to Christ:

> He said, "Then see the poorest of them all. See a poor body starved and bruised within an inch of death for Christ."
>
> He pulled his rags apart, and there beneath I saw no flesh but only bones with caked and sallow skin drawn tight. He wore an undercoat of rusty chains that must have weighed four stone. I saw where they had scraped him raw.
>
> "For every mouthful I don't eat or drink, Christ gets a mouthful more," he said. (109)

In contrast to the male ascetics, Godric's sister's self-starvation is an illness and symptom of her pining for her brother. Fearing his own incestuous attraction, Godric withdraws from her, and Burcwen begins to starve. William, their brother, describes her to Godric in words later echoed by Buechner in reference to his daughter's anorexia:

> I fear our sister ails. Some lettuce or a parsnip's all she takes for days on end. Water is her only drink.... Women's ways are ever strange. A radish now and then. She won't have meat or bread.... Her legs and arms become like sticks.... (154)

Godric remembers his feelings when he saw his sister suffering from anorexia: "Her eyes were fever-bright and she herself so lean she could have been a sailor shipwrecked on a raft for weeks. My bowels within me stirred for pity and remorse . . . " (154).

One summer night they consummate their illicit love, and William drowns looking for Burcwen. Guilt consumes them both. Godric takes up flagellation and self-torture in the Wear to chasten his flesh, and Burcwen's condition worsens. "She grew so thin her checks went hollow. The flesh around her mouth and eyes shrank back till you could see the skull beneath the skin" (159).

The psychological dynamics of anorexia and its connection to consuming familial love graphically portrayed between Godric and Burcwen reflect Buechner's experience at the time. Eleven years later in *Telling Secrets,* Buechner uses similar language to describe his daughter's near fatal anorexia nervosa and its effect on him while he wrote *Godric*:

> . . . she got more and more thin, . . . till she began to have the skull-like face and fleshless arms and legs of a victim of Buchenwald . . . . My anorectic daughter was in danger of starving to death, and without knowing it, so was I. I wasn't living my own life any more because I was so caught up in hers. (TS 23, 25)

Godric fears Burcwen has died, then learns she has gone to a convent. She briefly returns to collect her belongings accompanied by a nun whose presence prevents their communication. Godric sees Burcwen only one more time during an Easter mass at Durham. Years later, at her grave, Godric prays to her and makes peace. Her leaving for the convent has been her "salvation" and parallels Buechner's daughter's hospitalization which saved her life and also forced her father to release her, literally and emotionally.

The themes of loss and the ambivalence of friendship/kinship are central in *Godric*. The novel begins as Godric the aged hermit remembers the five friends he has lost over the years. Now as an old man he concludes,

> That's five friends, one for each of Jesu's wounds, and Godric bears their mark still on what's left of him as in their time they all bore his on them. What's friendship, when all's done, but the giving and taking of wounds?(7)

As Bruinooge and Engbers note:

> This rather bitter definition of friendship informs nearly every human relationship in the novel: character after character hurts the ones whom he or she loves in an attempt to love them. Aedlward, Godric's father, neglects his family working hard enough to feed them. Later in the novel, Godric becomes a sympathetic confidant for Hedwic, but Godric then ignores her so as not to spark de Granvill's jealousy: "So for love of her I wounded her by keeping from her sight, and thus my love stung both of us like hate" (*Godric* 86). (44, 45)

Buechner's understanding of the psychodynamics of family relationships is expressed in his astute portrayal of his characters. Throughout the novel, the relationship of Godric and his family, especially with his father and sister Burcwen, is a continual bearing of burdens and giving of wounds because of love: Godric almost drowns trying to hold onto a huge fish which he thinks of in terms "feeding a family all through spring" (15). As a youth, he is following in his father's footsteps in focusing only on physical needs. While being dragged under water by the porpoise, he "heard its voice, or so he thought, say, "Take and eat me, Godric, to thy soul's delight." Without equivocation, Godric says from this experience he "learned that it was Jesu saved him from the sea." The connection of the fish (ancient symbol of Christ) and the words are reminiscent of Christ's at the Last Supper and also at communion. Though desperately seeking physical food, Godric was given spiritual food, but at that time he did not appreciate it. Connected with his being saved from drowning was also his discovery of his sister's secret love. Right from the start, there is ambivalence in familial love. When Burcwen revives him on the beach by pressing her lips to his, he becomes aware of their incestuous attraction, and thereafter leaves her behind for he fears his own desires. She in turn becomes bitter and resentful, and their excessive love becomes tormenting and distancing whenever they are together.

The wounding nature of kinship, described as the burden of a heavy stone, is reiterated in the loss of his father:

> "Your father lies beneath a stone," old Aedwen mumbles, dozing at her wheel, and Godric thinks how it's a stone as well they're all beneath. The stone is need and hurt and gall and tongue-tied longing, for that's the stone that kinship always bears, yet the loss of it would press more grievous still. (54)

On their pilgrimage to Rome, Godric carries his mother when she is unable to walk on her own. This burden is light for him, however. When she is dying, she remembers this and asks if he will carry her. He soothingly replies he will.

Money and possessions are also a burden, a special concern for a monk who equates poverty with holiness and spirituality. Godric's ill-gotten gains are carried in heavy sacks, which he buries on Farne. After his baptism in the Jordan, he leaves the money at Elric's church, and then carries the ailing hermit who is a burden lighter than the heavy sacs he came with. By extension, these represent the material and emotional burdens all persons carry.

Having developed an increasing sense of his burden of guilt as he follows the steps of Christ through Jerusalem, Godric is relieved of its weight as he immerses himself in the Jordan.

> I waded out to where the water reached my neck, my beard outspread, my garments floating free. I let my hands bob up like corks. At sixteen stone or more, I felt I had, myself, no weight at all. The soul, set free from flesh at last, must know such peace. . . .
> And oh, the heart, the heart! . . . the untold weight of sin upon my heart was gone (104).

Here again, Buechner equates weightlessness with freedom from the flesh, which can signify freedom from physical weight, freedom from carnal desires, freedom from life itself in death, and freedom from sin. Three rivers portray these transitions. In the Wash, where he almost drowns under the physical weight of the fish, he is offered the spiritual food of Christ. In the Jordan baptism, his spiritual burdens are lifted and he accepts Christ's earlier offer, "Take, eat me, Godric, to thy soul's delight. Hold fast to him who gave his life for thee and thine" (104). In the icy Wear, to chasten his flesh, he dies daily, and finally as a type of last rites accepts the peace and blessing of God. Water has been used metaphorically to represent dying and rebirth, weightlessness and release from emotional burdens, and forgiveness of sins. These themes are intrinsic to the exceptional literary quality of the novel. They are also the issues Buechner was personally dealing with during this time in his life.

In therapy Buechner came to realize that much of his daughter's illness related to their codependent relationship, for he himself was wounded. He had held too tightly to his family, fearing a repetition of the loss of his father. By healing his own sense of paternal abandonment, and by realizing that his relationship with his father had never ended, he was able to come to a sense of peace, much like Godric experiences by the end of the novel. In therapy, as he was able to remember lost parts of his childhood and the feelings connected with them through written dialogue with his father using his left hand (TS 99-100). In the novel, similar resolutions are enacted. In prayer to Burcwen, at her grave, Godric says goodbye to his sister, prays for his father and brother, and comes to peace about these familial relationships.

Memory is torture for Godric, a hair shirt, an iron vest, the freezing ache of Wear. Thus even though the novel is resolved as Godric experiences the numbing blessing of Wear and the ultimate peace of death, the ambiguity and burdens of life are not easily dismissed. A modernist ambiguity remains reminiscent of the liberal narrative, the refusal to find simplistic ideological or psychological answers to life's difficulties. Yeats' "struggle with oneself" produces art. The concrete representation of the inner realities and feelings is thus what *Godric* does best, as indicated by the aged protagonist as he takes his last rites, his last immersion in the River Wear:

> How rough and yet how soft the river's touch!
> He falls about my shoulders like a silver shawl.
> He chills me to the marrow of my bones. He leaps
> and dances in the sun. He washes all my foulness
> off. And all the while, he slaps his rocky thighs
> and roars with mirth. (170)

Though aspects of the creative process can be appreciated in terms of literary qualities, they cannot be reduced to a formula. What ultimately is striking about Buechner's best work is the depth of characters that assume a life of their own. For Buechner, "Godric was my saint," an historical person with whom he identified. Yet, Buechner has defamiliarized his protagonist, locating him in a different time, setting, and even language from his own. Sometimes an author can be too involved, creating a thinly disguised autobiography rather than fiction, but in *Godric* Buechner has created a kind of "objective correlative" for his own experience. That which is most personal is most universal.

Concluding his second memoir *Now and Then,* Buechner describes the creative process as he wrote *Godric* which cannot be separated from the word *mystery*:

> Godric came as mysteriously alive for me as Bebb had and, with him, all the people he knew and the whole medieval world he lived in. I had Godric narrate his own life, and despite the problem of developing a language that sounded authentic on his lips without becoming impenetrably archaic, and despite the difficulties of trying to recapture a time and place so unlike my own, the book, like *Lion Country* before it, came so quickly and with such comparative ease that there were times when I suspected that maybe the old saint himself was not entirely uninvolved in the process, as, were I a saint and were somebody writing a book about me, I would not be entirely uninvolved in the process either.
>
> All sorts of adventures are described in the book because Godric's life was full of adventures, and I followed his life as accurately as I could; but Godric is a very old man as he tells his tale, and old age and the approach of death are very much in the back of his mind throughout. In this sense I think it was a book as prophetic, for me, as the Bebb books had been. It was prophetic in the sense that in its pages, more than half without knowing it, I was trying on various ways of growing old and facing death myself. As the years go by, Godric outlives, or is left behind by, virtually everybody he has ever loved—his sister, Burcwen; his shipmate, Roger Mouse; the two snakes, Tune and Fairweather, who for years were his constant companions; and the beautiful maid,

> Gillian, who appeared to him on the way back from his pilgrimage to Rome. But, although not without anguish, he is able to let them all go finally and to survive their going. His humanity and wit survive. His faith survives. He prays. He sins. He dreams. And one day not long before his death—bathing in the icy waters of the river Wear as for years he has bathed there, summer and winter, to chasten his flesh—he feels his arms and legs go numb, his pulse all but stop, and speaks these words both for himself and also for me:
>
> "Praise, praise!" I croak. Praise God for all that's holy, cold, and dark. Praise him for all we lose, for all the river of the years bears off. Praise him for stillness in the wake of pain. Praise him for emptiness. And as your race to spill into the sea, praise him yourself, old Wear. Praise him for dying and the peace of death.
>
> (Godric 96) (NT 107)
>
> What's lost is nothing to what's found," as Godric says, "and all the death that ever was, set next to life, would scarcely fill a cup." (Godric 96) (NT 109)

In the final scene in the River Wear, Godric releases his burdens, finding peace and joy. In accepting and letting go of his loss, he makes space for the love of God.

Remembering and accepting the loss of father, family and friends is at the heart of *Godric*, a novel that deals with overcoming loss and finding life's meaning in spite of pain. Buechner's unconscious psychological and spiritual struggles, when compressed and molded in the forge of the creative process, have produced a literary gem.

Notes

1 See "The Sins of the Fathers *Revisited*" in *The Critics Bear It Away: American Fiction and the Academy*. NY: Random House, 1992.

2 The term used by W. K. Wimsatt and Monroe C. Beardsley ("The Intentional Fallacy" (1946) reprinted in Wimsatt's *The Verbal Icon* (1964) was associated with interpretive errors in the New Criticism.

3 "Reference to the author's supposed purposes or else to the author's personal situation and state of mind in writing a text, is held to be a harmful mistake, because it diverts our attention to such 'external' matters as the author's biography, or psychological condition, or creative process, which we substitute for the proper critical concern with the 'internal' constitution and inherent value of the literary product. This claim, which was central in the New Criticism, has been strenuously debated, and has been reformulated by both of its original proponents.... A view acceptable to many traditional critics . . . is that in the exceptional instances—for example, in Henry James' prefaces to his novels—where we possess an author's express statement about his artistic intentions in a literary work, that statement should constitute evidence for an interpretive hypothesis, but should not in itself be determinative" (Abrams 90).

4 These comments may sound reminiscent of nineteenth-century psychological criticism which emphasized literature as an expression of the author's state of mind. Taking this emphasis to an extreme, romantic expressive criticism used the writer's personality to interpret his work and vice versa. Based on the assumption that the work directly reflects the writer's mental state, critics referred to literary works to assert biographical descriptions

of the author. "Critics of consciousness" stressed the value of reading literature as a way for the reader to enter into the writer's subjective experience. Objective literary qualities of the work were not as important as the psychological benefits. M. H. Abrams describes the "thoroughgoing proto-Freudian literary theory" proposed by John Keble in his lectures "On the Healing Power of Poetry" published in 1844:

"Poetry," Keble claimed, "is the indirect expression . . . of some overpowering emotion, or ruling taste, or feeling, the direct indulgence whereof is somehow repressed"; this repression is imposed by the author's sentiments of "reticence" and "shame"; the conflict between the need for expression and the compulsion to repress such self-revelation is resolved by the poet's ability to give "healing relief to secret mental emotion, yet without detriment to modest reserve" by a literary "art which under certain veils and disguises . . . reveals the fervent emotions of the mind"; and this disguised mode of self-expression serves as a safety valve, preserving men from madness." (264)

5 Leo Bebb and Mr. Golden's end remains a mystery when their plane bursts into flame and crashes yet no sign of them is found. They have either committed suicide, parachuted to safety or, like Elijah, been miraculously taken up to heaven in the fiery blaze.

6

The Son of Laughter: Healing the Shame that Binds

It was from the Jacob narratives in Genesis that... I saw, I think for the first time, that holiness is not something hazy and elusive that we know apart from the earth but something we can know only as it wells up out of the earth, out of people even as clay-footed as Jacob, the trickster and crook, out of places as elemental as the river Jabbok, where he wrestled in darkness with a Stranger who was no stranger, out of events as seamy as the time he gulled his half-blind father out of Esau's blessing. "See, the smell of my son is as the smell of a field which the Lord has blessed," [Gen. *27:27*] old Isaac says as he lays his hands upon Jacob, and there it is all in a moment: Jacob betrays his brother, dupes his father, all but chokes on his own mendacity, yet the smell of him is the smell of blessing because God, no less than Isaac, has chosen to bless him in spite of everything. Jacob reeks of holiness. His life is as dark, fertile, and holy as the earth itself. He is himself a bush that burns with everything, both fair and foul, that a man burns with. Yet he is not consumed because God out of his grace will not consume him. (NT 19-20)

The Son of Laughter represents Buechner's most conscious use of psychological dynamics to reveal and explain spiritual truths. Whereas *The Book of Bebb* and *Godric* arose spontaneously, "from the place where dreams come from," and incorporated almost on a subconscious level the psychological and spiritual issues Buechner was experiencing at the time he wrote them, *The Son of Laughter* germinated in Buechner's mind over a long period of time and incorporates a more conscious approach to psycho-spirituality. This approach is apparent in the interrelated issues the protagonist must deal with in himself: moral ambivalence and toxic shame.[1] As Jacob works through his psychological issues by revisiting his hurt trail, he comes to experience his love story and the spiritual renewal implied in his name change from Jacob (Heels) to Israel (one who strives with God and man and perseveres). Buechner thus uses the events provided by the Jacob narratives in Genesis to explore the process of psychological and spiritual growth as an Old Testament saint listens to his life.

Buechner was fascinated by the character of Jacob long before he had articulated the concept of listening to his life or experienced psychotherapy. While preparing a study of the Pentateuch for an Old Testament class at Union Seminary in the 1950s, he was struck by the fair/foul duality in the biblical Jacob, and the concept

> that holiness is not something hazy and elusive that we know apart from the earth but something we can know only as it wells up out of the earth, out of people even as clay-footed as Jacob . . . because God, no less than Isaac, has chosen to

> bless him in spite of everything. Jacob reeks of holiness. His life is as dark, fertile, and holy as the earth itself. He is himself a bush that burns with everything, both fair and foul, that a man burns with. Yet he is not consumed because God out of his grace will not consume him. (NT 19-20)

Buechner saw Jacob as representative of all poignantly fallible human beings whom God chose to bless in spite of their moral weakness and failures. For Buechner this is the meaning of grace, and in the story of Jacob he sees the archetypal pattern of God's postlapsarian interaction with Adam and Eve in Genesis 3 and in all subsequent divine interventions throughout the Old and New Testaments. His attraction to Jacob was the seeming paradox of grace: God's strength is perfected in weakness, and He chooses to bless those who sense their dire need. Buechner came to conclude with his seminary professor James Muilenburg:

> Until you can read the story of Adam and Eve, of Abraham and Sarah, of David and Bathsheba, as your own story . . . you have not really understood it. The Bible . . . is a book finally about ourselves, our own apostasies, our own battles and blessings. (NT 21)

Forty years later when Buechner wrote *The Son of Laughter* (1993), in retelling the story of Jacob, the son of Isaac (which means laughter), he was also writing his own story and the story of all fallible human beings. To do this Buechner filled in the skeletal plot of the Jacob narratives with the flesh and blood of psychological dynamics. By this time he had been in therapy himself and was aware of the psychological dynamics of toxic shame, which he used to shape Jacob's character in *The Son of Laughter.*

Like Godric, Buechner's Jacob is an old man who revisits the events of his life in an autobiographical reminiscence. As the first-person narrator, Jacob remembers his life in flashbacks, reexperiencing acts of deceit and feelings of fear, guilt and shame. Jacob's sense of shame is a recurring theme, a pulsating presence that runs through his past, which must be faced before he can experience his love story. Like Godric (and Antonio Parr to a lesser degree), Jacob has become increasingly aware of the ways God has been faithful and blessed him when he least deserved it. In *The Son of Laughter* Buechner portrays the excruciatingly painful experience of shame and guilt in the life of an Old Testament Patriarch who became a hero of the faith,. The psychological dynamics of shame are explored and its resolution includes a process of psychological and spiritual growth as well as forgiveness of sin.

In reference to this unique psychological-spiritual approach in *The Son of Laughter*, Joseph Sendry commends Buechner's "psychological analysis that is unsettling for its acuity." Citing the literary reasons the Conference on Christianity and Literature chose *The Son of Laughter* its *belles lettres* book of the year for 1993, Sendry calls it

> a novel of singular imaginative power, distinguished both for its literary achievement and as a searching reflection on the meaning of faith. . . . . Buechner's literary achievement derives from a sustained narrative mastery that propels readers forward as if they were entering new fictional territory. . . . we are made to see, and hear, and touch, and smell, and feel a world remote from ours temporally, spatially, and culturally. . . . Nor does it stop with a psychological analysis that is unsettling for its acuity. Nor even with the evocation of moral grandeur, teased convincingly from flawed human agents. His power as a novelist is tested to the utmost in meeting the challenge of showing the intrusion of the divine into human life. (378)

The Son of Laughter: Healing the Shame That Binds

Buechner's "psychological analysis that is unsettling for its acuity" sets up the convincing "intrusion of the divine into human life" which Sendry notes, the psychologically attuned spirituality, which is the hallmark of Buechner's writing. This psychological understanding of human ambivalence and fair/foul motivations and behaviors developed in Buechner's novels over the years. The psychological effects of guilt and shame which in Buechner's Jacob are articulated through his thoughts and feelings, in his earlier characters were acted out in negative ways: bewilderment and despair (Tristram Bone), lying and hysteria (Elizabeth Poor), isolation and ambivalence (Ansel Gibbs), running away (Roonie Vail, Theodore Nicolet), pathological sexuality (Bebb's indecent exposure), alcoholism (Lucille Bebb) and suicide (Rudy Tripp, Lucille Bebb).

Moving from psychological analysis to the intrusion of the divine, Buechner is no less convincing. Roonie Vail ultimately deals with her guilt through spiritual confession and forgiveness. Antonio Parr draws on Bebb's faith to become aware of spiritual transcendence and comes to accept himself and his responsibilities with "something like grace." Through a process of asceticism, self-therapy, and confession of sin, Godric experiences peace and joy. In *The Son of Laughter* in his new identity as Israel, Jacob accepts God's unconditional love and is freed from the toxic shame that had him bound. In all Buechner's novels, shame and guilt are psychological and spiritual conditions that affect both heroic and non-heroic characters. They all experience guilt but their reactions differ. Buechner's more spiritually mature characters use various forms of self-therapy, listening to their lives and working through the painful past to discover their divine love story, which leads to confession and forgiveness and healing.

More than any other character, Heels is a man plagued by shame, an important issue in contemporary personality theory, replacing Freud's emphasis on the sexual instinct. According to Michael Lewis, professor of pediatrics, psychiatry, and psychology at the University of Medicine and Dentistry of New Jersey, and author of *Shame: The Exposed Self*:

> The species-specific feeling of shame is central in our lives. Shame, more than sex or aggression is responsible for controlling our psychic course. ... Our internal struggles are not battles between instincts and reality, but conflicts that typically involve the understanding and negotiating of shame, its elicitors, and its frequency. (3)

Recent popular books such as John Bradshaw's *Healing the Shame That Binds You* (1988) and literature from the recovery movement emphasize the connection of shame, addictions, and dysfunctional family systems. In his last memoir *Telling Secrets*, Buechner notes the need for recovery from the effects of a dysfunctional family when he describes the help he received from Alanon, a group for adult children of alcoholics connected with Alcoholics Anonymous (89-95). In the recovery movement, emphasis is placed on understanding codependency and on the need for inner healing from toxic shame.

Lewis, Allen, Bradshaw, and most other therapists distinguish between shame and guilt.

> Shame can be distinguished from guilt: a total self-failure vis-a-vis a standard produces shame, while a specific self-failure results in guilt. (Lewis 9)
>
> Shame can be defined simply as the feeling we have when we evaluate our actions, feelings, or behavior, and conclude that we have done wrong. It encompasses the whole of ourselves; it generates a wish to hide, to disappear, or even to die. (Lewis 2)

As Allen often states, "Guilt is when you feel you have made a mistake; shame is when you feel you are a mistake."

Buechner's Jacob is a man consumed by toxic shame which colors his identity and worldview. The causes and physical manifestations of Heels' shame reflect a contemporary psychological understanding:

> Shame is the product of a complex set of cognitive activities: the evaluation of an individual's actions in regard to her standards, rules, and goals, and her global evaluation of the self. The phenomenological experience of the person having shame is that of a wish to hide, disappear, or die. Shame is a highly negative and painful state that also results in the disruption of ongoing behavior, confusion in thought, and an inability to speak. The physical action accompanying shame includes a shrinking of the body, as though to disappear from the eye of the self or the other. (Lewis 2)

Though understanding shame as a central psychodynamic factor has become prominent in the second half of the twentieth century, shame as a powerful emotion with specific characteristics has long been acknowledged. In *Expression of Emotion in Man and Animals,* Charles Darwin described the overt physical manifestation of shame with an emphasis on the facial expression: head averted or bent down with the eyes wavering or turned away (now referred to as gaze avert), and facial blushing. Interestingly, to illustrate this, Darwin cites the Old Testament prophet Ezra, "Oh my God, I am ashamed and I blush to lift my head to thee, oh God!" Darwin associates shame with blushing and a desire for concealment (Lewis 22). Shame has long been observed as a common human response, but only in the last half of the twentieth century has it been studied as a major component of personality theory.

Representing the essence of his psycho-spiritual approach,

Buechner's definition of psychotherapy discussed in chapter one uses the Genesis account of Adam and Eve's hiding after the Fall to portray the human response to shame, and God's divinely therapeutic intervention. "Having a new understanding of who they are and a new strength to draw on for what lies before them to do now" (WD 106) follows their guilty admission of where they are and what they have done. They have come to face themselves, in their nakedness and shame, and have received a new identity as forgiven human beings with new strength in God's continuing provision and providence. This emphasis on the role of shame as causing separation between humans and the Creator is central to Buechner's psychological-spiritual paradigm.

In *The Son of Laughter*, Heels is a man bound by toxic shame, as his self-depreciating name indicates. As in the biblical narrative, he is given the new name Israel when he is wounded and blessed during his struggle with the Lord (Genesis 32:24-31). What the biblical account portrays in deed, Buechner explains using psychological dynamics. Using his imagination, historical research into the customs of the time, and psychological insights, Buechner provides details which the biblical account only implies or omits altogether. In these details, Buechner brings the heroic down to a human level, showing that Jacob, though a Hebrew patriarch with a direct call from God, was in many ways similar to a twentieth-century seeker enmeshed in the ambivalence of God's revelation and the paradox of his own human fallibility. A comparison of the Jacob narratives with the additions and omissions in *The Son of Laughter* illuminates Buechner's insights as a writer, therapist and theologian, as he creates a psychological-spiritual retelling of the scriptures.

The most significant change Buechner makes in the biblical account is the use of a first-person narrator, the method he began with *Alphabet of Grace* and continued in *The Book of Bebb* and *Godric*. To portray his subjective experience, which contains a mixture of human fallibility and divine blessing, Buechner has Jacob narrate the story of his own life. Whereas the biblical account is told by a third-person narrator, *The Son of Laughter* is Jacob's non-chronological reminiscence about the past. Jacob's first-person narration allows a subjective, spontaneous account which reveals psychological dynamics about the protagonist and the other characters. As mentioned previously, agnostic narrator Antonio Parr's inner dilemmas affect the telling of his story and the reader's perceptions of Bebb, as Parr moves from skepticism to questioning to quasi-faith. First-person narration gives *The Son of Laughter* characteristics of a confessional like Buechner's novel *Godric*, in which the penitent protagonist admits sins and impure motives, and accepts responsibility for harmful consequences of his behavior. The first-person narrator is also reminiscent of the self-exposure of a patient in psychotherapy, as the patient reviews his or her life, seeking to find connections, recognize inner conflicts and defenses, and understand familial patterns. The importance of memory in both psychotherapy and confession leading to forgiveness of sin is implicit in Buechner's use of a first-person narrator who is engaged in the process of listening to his life.

The psychological difference made by having the subjective experience of the first-person narrator in *The Son of Laughter* is highlighted when seen in contrast to the Hebrew scriptures. In Genesis the same basic events are recounted by an invisible third person, in a voice that is authoritative and omniscient. In the biblical account, God's words are clear, direct communications, provided verbatim as statements of fact. In Buechner, the "word of the Lord" is presented more naturally: the words of God are whispered in Jacob's ear or imprinted on his consciousness.

Secondly, because it is his subjective account, what Jacob does not hear is not included. Thus, in *The Son of Laughter* we are never told the prophetic message God gives to Rebekah when she inquires of the Lord about the twins struggling in her womb before the birth of Jacob and Esau. However, in the biblical narrative it is recorded:

> And the Lord said to her,

> "Two nations are in your womb;
> And two peoples shall be separated from your body;
> And one people shall be stronger than the other;
> And the older shall serve the younger."
>
> Genesis 25:23

Instead, in *The Son of Laughter* we hear Jacob's story as Jacob remembers what he experienced at the time before he had the perspective of a lifetime. He must take one step at a time, not knowing the future or the outcome. Often it is only in retrospect that he sees the hand of God working on his behalf.

As in *Godric*, first-person narration in *The Son of Laughter* works on a number of levels: Jacob is undergoing a kind of psychotherapeutic process at the end of his life as he relives his hurt trail, reexperiencing the pain, but now aware of the love story it reveals. At the same time Buechner is retelling his own experience of pain and loss, including insights gained from therapy. Buechner's inductive autobiographical impulse based on listening to his life parallels his descriptive theology as the way he views God's revelation, whether through an individual life or through scripture. As Buechner interprets the interaction of Adam and Eve with God after the fall as embodying principles of psychotherapy, so he writes *The Son of Laughter* to portray Jacob wrestling with himself and God, as he seeks to answer the same questions God asked Adam and Eve: "Where are you?" and "What have you done?"

As the focus on his name change from Jacob to Israel makes clear, however, the most central question he must answer is "Who am I?" In this regard his name, a reflection of his real inner self, is significant. As in the scriptural account, at his birth he is named Jacob or Heels, because he was delivered second, grabbing onto the heels of the first born twin, Esau, which Buechner interprets to mean hairy. The Hebrew word Jacob means supplanter or heel grabber and Buechner stresses this aspect of his personality by having Jacob refer to himself as Heels. By using the translated name Heels in reference to Jacob, Buechner is also juxtaposing the colloquial expression for "cad," which aptly fits his protagonist. Thus name change significantly reflects changing identity. Correspondence of name and identity change was also seen in other novels. Tono became the Reverend Antonio Parr and Godric moved from being called Deric to his Christian name with its multiple possible etymologies, showing that there had been internal character changes but their mixed identity never totally disappeared.

Jacob's caddish, manipulative identity as Heels is indicative of his psychological motivation. Because he is living with a sense of guilt, his dominant personality traits are shame and fear. What first strikes the reader is Jacob's name for God, the Fear. Although this term is used in the Jacob narratives twice (but only in reference to "the Fear of Isaac"), the term "God" or "the Lord" is more often found in the Hebrew scriptures. In Buechner, however, it is as the Fear that God reveals himself. This is evident in the first chapter when Jacob first mentions the Fear in connection with the buried gods. Jacob says,

> It wasn't long afterward, when Laban had gone, that I got rid of them [Laban's household idols which Rachael had stolen]. It was for the Fear's sake I did it. The Fear came to me in the night and whispered words of hope into my ear. He told me that he loved me as he had loved Laughter, my father, before me and Abraham, my grandfather, before that. He repeated the ancient promises that never fail to frighten me with their beauty just as the Fear himself never fails to frighten me. (6)

The corresponding passage in Genesis 35:1-4 states simply:

> Then God said to Jacob, "Arise, go up to Bethel, and live there; and make an altar there to

God who appeared to you when you fled from your brother Esau." So Jacob said to his household and to all who were with him, "Put away the foreign gods which are among you and purify yourselves, and change your garments; and let us arise and go up to Bethel; and I will make an altar there to God, who answered me in the day of my distress, and has been with me wherever I have gone."

In Buechner, Heels' primary motivation is fear. He buries the gods out of fear (even though he is still afraid of them as well), and he is frightened not only by the Fear but also by his promises. In contrast, in the Jacob narratives Jacob acts out of simple obedience. The narratives create a stronger sense of authority from the Lord, citing positive and direct imperatives in the voice of the Almighty, as opposed to a less substantial, more subjective interpretation of what was said "in his ear." The biblical Jacob is far more certain and confident—God answered him in his day of distress and is with him wherever he goes.

In contrast, Buechner's Heels is filled with a sense of his own shame, reflected in his fearful relationship with the Fear. By chapter four, we learn even as a youth, he was sure the Fear was angry because he had shrewdly acquired Esau's birthright (33). Jacob blamed himself for the fact there was no rain, which caused a famine, and he dreaded lest the casting of the two stones would reveal his guilt to his father. In the scriptures there is no mention of any second thoughts on the part of Jacob, nor are there two stones for divination to determine the cause of the famine. In fact, Esau's forfeiting his birthright for a mess of pottage is attributed to his own impulsiveness and shortsightedness. Genesis 25 states simply:

> And when Jacob had cooked stew, Esau came in from the field and he was famished; and Esau said to Jacob, Please let me have a swallow of

> that red stuff there, for I am famished [lit. weary]."
> Therefore his name was called Edom [lit. red].
> But Jacob said, "First sell me your birthright,"
> And Esau said, "Behold, I am about to die, so of what use then is the birthright to me?'
> And Jacob said, "First swear to me"; so he swore to him, and sold his birthright to Jacob.
> Then Jacob gave Esau bread and lentil stew; and he ate and drank, and rose and went on his way. Thus Esau despised his birthright. (Genesis 25:29-34)

Significantly, the concluding comment offered in the biblical text is the judgment against Esau: "Thus Esau despised his birthright."

In contrast, Buechner's Heels continually battles his guilty conscience as he remembers how he took advantage of his brother. His sense of shame casts a long shadow coloring everything: "I felt my eyes puddling. I not only knew he would let me do it, but I also knew I would do it and would like doing it, such a sad and shameful thing" (25). When the deal is made, Heels gives his brother the stew with the words, "Take and eat then." Here is a subtle play on the words Christ used when he gave his disciples the symbols of his body and blood at the Last Supper, "Take, eat. This is my body of the new covenant. Do this as often as you do it in remembrance of me." Perhaps Buechner here is ironically echoing the words of Christ who freely shared his birthright with his disciples, the opposite of what Heels has done. Heels' ambivalence is captured in the final sentences of the episode as he sums up the exchange between the two brothers:

> That is how Heels got what Heels wanted and Hairy got what Hairy wanted. As to which of them got the better of the bargain, who can say? (28).

Nowhere is the effect of his shame core more apparent than in Buechner's account of Jacob's deception to procure the blessing of his father Isaac (corresponding to Genesis 27:27-29). In retrospect, Jacob recalls his experience of toxic shame when as Heels he deceived his father:

> The last time I saw him as the father I had always known was the day I pulled the wool over his blind eyes. . . . I was Jacob still—Heels, heel-grabber. . . . I did what my mother badgered me into doing. I did it because she badgered me, did it because if someone had turned the stone of my heart, he would have found beetles there. I moved from lie to lie like a jackal stalking his prey from bush to bush. (80)

As he recounts the circumstances of Isaac's giving him the blessing, his focus is on the punishment he anticipates from God: "Thus I fouled the Fear's name with the filth of my lie and waited in terror. Already I felt the Fear strangling me" (82).

As Laughter eats the stew, instead of a sense of relief, terror and paranoia consume Jacob coloring his view of his father, the Fear, and nature:

> It was Laughter I feared—the look in his sightless eyes as it dawned on him what I was up to. Unless of course he already knew what I was up to. Most of all it was the Fear I feared. The blessing I was stealing from my father was the Fear's blessing. I knew that the Fear too was within earshot. The sun had turned red. It was the Fear's angry eye. I heard the rustle of his wings behind me if the Fear has wings. If the Fear has leathery talons fierce enough to pinion a sheep or a man, has an eagle's creaking cackle. (83)

As Heels is about to receive Laughter's blessing, his shame overcomes him emotionally and physically:

> I could feel my own face burn as I knelt there with his hands upon me. My face did not burn with light like a god's. Shame was what burned it, a hot shame fragrant as kids stewed with leeks and melon. I was scorched. I was ashamed for my mother's cunning and my brother's dull wits. Most of all I was ashamed for myself. I prayed to feel the great claws sink into my flesh, the peck and dazzle of the merciless beak granting me the mercy of death. (85)

Like Godric's penance (flagellation and bathing in the freezing river Wear) after his sin, Jacob's reaction is to feel the need to be punished and a desire to die, the ultimate defense in the face of toxic shame. Because Heels is shame based, when old Isaac utters the words, "Cursed be everyone who curses you, and blessed be everyone who blesses you," Heels negatively responds with a self-imposed penance which affects the way he retrospectively views his life: "I was doubly cursed then because I cursed myself. I made enemies of my father and brother. I became a fugitive. Twenty years I slaved for Laban. I lost my beloved on the road to Ephrath" (86).

Because Heels' shame casts a negative light even on favorable circumstances, for him the blessing "was far more terrible still" (86). He compares it to a runaway camel that nothing can stop and concludes, "It was not I who ran off with my father's blessing. It was my father's blessing that ran off with me" (86). As an old man, looking back at his life, Jacob remembers his hurt trail that although blessed, was painful and filled with its share of self-imposed curses. Through introspection, characteristic more of the patient in analysis than the biblical patriarch, Buechner gives Jacob self-knowledge of what his sense of shame has cost him.

In the original narrative, Genesis 27, there is no mention of Jacob's introspection or any sense of shame; rather, when he obeys his mother in deceiving his father, his only concern is that the ruse may not work. Once he receives Isaac's blessing, he has no qualms (or any other feelings for that matter) about what he has done. He deceives his father, receives the blessing, and leaves before Esau returns.

While adding an extensive portrayal of Heels' shame, Buechner also omits a significant episode contained in the Jacob narrative right after Rebekah learns of Esau's plan to kill Jacob and she tells him to flee to her brother Laban. The Genesis narrative then states,

> And Rebekah said to Isaac, "I am tired of living because of the daughters of Heth [Esau's pagan wives]. If Jacob takes a wife from the daughters of Heth, like these, from the daughters of the land, what good will my life be to me?"
>
> So Isaac called Jacob and blessed him and charged him, and said to him, "You shall not take a wife from the daughters of Canaan. Arise, go to Paddan-aram, to the house of Bethuel your mother's father; and from there take to yourself a wife from the daughters of Laban your mother's brother. And may God Almighty bless you and make you fruitful and multiply you, that you may become a company of peoples. May He also give you the blessing of Abraham, to you and your descendants with you, that you may possess the land of your sojournings, which God gave to Abraham. (Genesis 27:46-28:4)

Thus in the biblical narrative, Jacob leaves with the conscious blessing of Isaac. He is acting out of obedience to his father and mother in seeking a wife (unlike Esau). The extensive passage of his introspective guilt before the dream of the stone stair is also absent in the original narrative.

In the protagonist's psychological development, however, the culmination of Heels' shame comes as he leaves home, fleeing from Esau at his mother's insistence, to seek refuge with his uncle Laban in Haran. Buechner adds the warning from Rebekah as the last words to her son, "Watch out for Laban," which though not in the scriptural account, foreshadows the problematic side of Jacob's heritage. Buechner also accentuates Jacob's soul-searching introspection:

> For the first days I traveled, my eyes were fixed only inward.... I saw the fat, milky-eyed face of my father... I saw Esau's face.... What I drank from the small, pale puddle of my mother's face—the painted eyes and puffed cheeks, the rabbity teeth—was bitter as death...I saw over my head an emptiness that had no end. I saw darkness. I heard silence deeper than the kingdom of the dead. I knew that this was the way the face of the Fear appears to those who have committed abominations in his sight, and I shuddered beneath it. (91-92)

As guilt and shame overcome Heels, he is simultaneously climbing a steep hill covered with rocks that resemble grave markers. The outer landscape reflects his inner experience as he feels a "cruel pounding" in his head as he climbs.

> The pain was a voice telling me over and over again that I had made some stupid mistake—I was following the wrong path...Sometimes the pain was a face. It was Esau's face. He was watching me as I climbed. When I got to a certain place he would kill me..... (92)

In this state of paranoia bordering on psychosis, Jacob reaches a level place and lies down with a flat stone under his head. Here he dreams of the stone stair—the ladder to heaven—where God appears, confirming the blessing he received from Isaac. When Heels is in deepest despair, God reveals his undeserved grace.

After the dream of the angels ascending and descending and God's pronouncement of blessing and promise, Jacob responds by restating God's promise if he is willing to trust him. In the original scriptures, Jacob's statement seems to be a positive acceptance of God's covenant. In *The Son of Laughter*, the same "if, then" response is interpreted in Heels' memory as a *quid pro quo* bargain which reveals his self-seeking propensity:

> What I spoke to the Fear then at the pillar I have shuddered often to remember. Instead of the anger I awaited, what his star words brought me down the stone stairs was promise. He promised me the land I lay on.
>
> He promised that from Haran he would bring me home. He promised to be with me and to keep me all my days.
>
> What I spoke to him at his altar was IF.
>
> "If you will be with me and will keep me in this way that I go," I said, "if you will give me bread to eat and clothing to wear so that I come again to my father's house in peace, then you shall be my God . . ." Those were my words. Even with him I hedged and bargained. (95)

Buechner accentuates the subtleties of the text (interpreted as a hedging, conditional promise), to imply a manipulative response which Heels is ashamed of when he remembers it.

Thus Buechner supplies Jacob with psychological self-awareness and sensitivity. When he steals Esau's birthright, Jacob is ashamed that he duped his brother. Suspecting that the Fear is angry with him, he wonders if it is his fault there is no rain (34). In the novel he analyzes his motives for betraying his brother (76), and he experiences shame when he remembers his deception of Isaac (81) and believes he has fouled the Fear's name (82). Later he feels guilty about his treatment of Leah, thinking, "Perhaps it was because I wronged her for many years the way I had also wronged him" (138). Even after he has received the Fear's blessing, he continues to feel shame (161). The biblical narratives portray the same actions as Buechner's Jacob, but there is no mention that Jacob feels guilty about his behavior or is consumed by shame.

Shame reinforces Jacob's fear. Buechner portrays Heels living in the House of Fear in terms of Allen's psychological paradigm. Jacob refers to God as "the Fear." He fears his brother and his father. He relates at length the trauma Isaac experienced when he was almost sacrificed by Abraham, a trauma which had left its mark on Isaac, and which is always in the back of Jacob's mind as a potential fate for himself. Jacob knows he does not deserve the blessing he has usurped, so he is always afraid that he will be punished. This is in keeping with the confessional genre in which the penitent recounts what he has done, admits impure motives underlying any seemingly noble actions and seeks forgiveness.

Drawing on lessons from the recovery movement, Buechner connects Heels' toxic shame to his dysfunctional family background. He emphasizes the acute psychological trauma and transgenerational familial patterns based on manipulation and deceit which have shaped Jacob. Although in both the Hebrew scriptures and the novel Rebekah persuades her favorite son Jacob to deceive his father to get the blessing, Buechner expands her manipulative character to include other incidents which reveal a dysfunctional family pattern.

In *The Son of Laughter*, Rebekah is constantly scheming. She persuades her husband to lie that she is his sister (whereas in the Hebrew scriptures, Isaac makes the decision on his own). Buechner details Rebekah's use of makeup and mannerisms to attract and manipulate the men of Gerar. A deceitful, conniving person, she persuades Jacob to trick Isaac into blessing him. Throughout the novel her marital relationship with Isaac is problematic, exhibiting constant tension and a running battle of the wills.

The incidents of Laban's manipulation, in tricking Jacob into marrying Leah, and then changing his wages, is well documented in the scriptures. However, Buechner accentuates Laban's manipulative personality (calling Jacob "darling," and being overly affectionate) as he has Laban's sister, Rebekah. He expands the account of Laban's attachment to the idols as a way to gain an edge over other people, to know secrets only the gods reveal, and to trick others. Buechner details Laban's deception in switching Leah for Rachel, in bargaining with Jacob over the years he is to work, and in cheating him of his share of the spotted goats and sheep. Laban's daughter Rachel stole the family idols and deceived her father when he came in search of them. Buechner pulls together these incidents to underscore the deceitful traits that even Rachel shares. In light of the manipulative, deceitful familial characteristics of his mother, uncle, and wife, no wonder Jacob is a supplanter. Thus the fallible, unfavorable, and sinful qualities of Jacob and his family are underscored to show how deceit is ingrained in the human race. As he saw in his earliest reading of the Jacob narratives, Buechner determines to make the clay-footed foulness of Heels tangible to the reader. There can be no doubt that Jacob indeed burns with everything, both fair and foul, that a man burns with. Here is no plaster saint, yet, like Graham Greene's whiskey priest, he is blessed because God has chosen to bless him.

In addition to patterns of manipulation and deceit, Buechner portrays the weakness of Jacob's father, Isaac, whose name "Laughter" was given because Sarah laughed when she heard she would have a son in her old age. Whereas the Bible is silent on the emotional impact that Isaac experienced as a result of his being offered as a sacrifice, Buechner portrays its lasting traumatic effect. The second chapter "The Ram in the Thicket" is a flashback to the time Isaac was taken to be sacrificed by his father Abraham. We gain a double perspective from a psychological point of view: Jacob is remembering the painful and humiliating time when Isaac told him the terrible events of that day, and he also remembers the events themselves. Jacob recalls,

> Laughter said, "Heels, I am telling this to you, not to your brother...Now I will finish my story," Laughter said. He started to weep.
> It was the worst moment of my life up till then. I was so ashamed of Laughter's weeping that I thought I was going to be sick. I wanted to run out of the tent so I would not have to see his tears. Instead I stayed in the tent to punish him by seeing them. I stayed in the tent to punish myself by seeing them. It was slovenly, shameful weeping. Dribble ran out of Laughter's nose. His mouth ran spittle. He bared his gums in an ugly, comic way. He blubbered like a woman. His whole thick frame shook. I squatted by the smoking dung staring at him. (15)

Thus we see the effect the telling had on Jacob—he feels ashamed at the grotesque scene and his father's humiliation in telling him. At the same time, we come to understand why Isaac is so timid, so bullied by Rebekah, so "deferential" toward others. He has been psychologically traumatized (castrated) by the experience of his father's broken trust. The chapter ends as the extent of the trauma, about which Isaac has never before spoken, is apparent:

> He [Isaac] said, "When my mother heard what Abraham had nearly done to her son, she was dead within the year. What killed her? You tell me. And when you tell me what killed her,

> then you can tell me what killed me. Oh Heels, Heels!" he cried out. "My son, Jacob!"
> He said, "I was not always the way you see me now." (19-20)

Rather than a glorious portrayal of Isaac's unwavering faith and the triumphant intervention of the angel to stop Abraham and provide the ram for sacrifice, the focus is on Isaac as a broken man, still traumatized by what he experienced as a youth. The way the episode is told establishes the frightening relationship Isaac had with his own father and the Fear, and helps explain the transgenerational heritage which has left Jacob fearful, scheming, and shame based. Coming from this dysfunctional family, Jacob has been traumatized as well. Buechner's vivid, grotesque description of Isaac shows that even the Old Testament Patriarchs are human and fragmented.

The narratives of Jacob and Joseph, comprising the second half of the book of Genesis (chapters 25 through 50), relate the main events in the life of Jacob and Joseph in chronological order. Similarly, *The Son of Laughter* is divided into two parts: "The Promising" deals with Jacob's reminiscences about his life as he comes to recognize the promise and call of God on his life while simultaneously coming to know himself. "The Dreaming" focuses on Joseph in Egypt and the family's ultimate reunification.

In terms of Buechner's psychological spirituality, Part I "The Promising" is the most revealing. It deals with the ambivalent events in Jacob's life, told by Jacob in non-chronological order, with missing sections, and missing details which are not provided until later. The structure of Part I reflects Jacob's psychological journey, as he moves from shame and fear to acceptance and love. This development is not neatly linear, and Buechner uses an inverted chronology to emphasize incidents from different vantagepoints, depending on how Jacob is remembering them. For example, rather than begin the novel with his birth, Jacob begins with the burial of the household gods. This tells the reader something about how Jacob views his life, although its significance to Jacob is not apparent until later. When this incident is mentioned in scripture (Genesis 35:2-4), it is a brief event without explanation, occurring between Jacobs' sons' vengeance on the men of Shechem and the death of Rachel during the birth of Benjamin. In the novel "The Buried Gods" is chapter one, but Jacob does not relate the context or its significance until chapter 17 "The Red Heifer." This chapter relates Jacob's sacrifice to atone for the guilt of his sons and himself. Here also the significance of the buried gods is clarified as Jacob recounts the context omitted previously explaining the differences between the Fear and the pagan gods, a key lesson which as Israel he has finally come to understand:

> The unclean blood no longer clung to our hands, but the small gods clung still to our hearts. They clung with silver fingers, with fingerless hands of wood and baked clay. Like rats, the gods gibbered in our hearts about the rich gifts they have for giving to us. The Gods give rain. The swelling udder they give and the sweet fig, the plump ear of grain, the ooze of oil. They give sons. To Laban they gave cunning. They give their names as the Fear, at the Jabbok, refused me his when I asked it, and a god named is a god summoned. The Fear comes when he comes. It is the Fear who summons. The gods give in return for your gifts to them: the strangled dove, the burnt ox, the first fruit. There are those who give them their firstborn even, the child bound to the altar for knifing as Abraham bound Isaac til the Fear of his mercy bade the urine-soaked old man unbind him. The Fear gives to the empty-handed, the empty-hearted, as to me from the stone stair he gave promise and blessing, and gave them also to Isaac before me, to Abraham before Isaac, all of

us wanderers only, herdsmen and planters moving with the seasons as gales of dry sand move with the wind. In return it is only the heart's trust that the Fear asks. Trust him though you cannot see him and he has no silver hand to hold. Trust him though you have no name to call him by, though out of the black night he leaps like a stranger to cripple and bless.

It was to cleanse our hearts of every other trust but trust in the Fear that I made them bury their gods and Laban's gods in the hole under the oak near Abraham's tumbled altar limed with bird drippings. (184)

By starting *The Son of Laughter in medias res* with the incident of the buried gods, Buechner is focusing on an event which we later learn reveals Israel's inner transformation. Not until chapter 17, "The Red Heifer," is the significance of the burial of the foreign gods expressed. From being one who based all his dealings on trade, trickery, manipulation, as did the foreign gods, Israel has come to realize he is empty handed. No longer is his relationship to God or others based on what he can get or what he can give. Now he has realized life itself is grace. His relationship with the Fear has changed from one of wanting to use God for his own ends, to fearing His reprisals, to believing in and trusting His grace. Israel's emotions have moved from fear and shame to trust and acceptance as he has come to an end of himself and his own manipulative strivings. He knows he is empty-handed, yet in spite of his failings, God has chosen to bless him. Burying the gods represents his commitment to follow the one God fully. Unlike his reaction after the dream of the stone stair, when in response to the Fear's promise, his obedience was conditional on further evidence of God's provision ("if you will do this, then I will do that"), now his mature relationship is based on trust, even when he cannot see the tangible representation of God or know His name. Thus the burial of the gods reveals the change that has made Jacob into Israel.

Although the extent of the meaning of Jacob's burial of the gods is not revealed in chapter one, what is emphasized is the connection of the idols to human desires, the things his uncle Laban "lusted to know" (4). Their blessing is based on manipulation and exchange. "They all had names, but I have forgotten them," the novel begins. One cannot summon a god without knowing his name, for names represent identity. At the end of the chapter, Jacob admits the "fair and foul" mixture of ambivalence in himself:

> When I say that I have forgotten their names, I mean that I cannot remember their names without trying. There are also times when I cannot forget their names without trying.
>
> Maybe they also remember me. Who knows about gods? Maybe they have seen every step I have taken ever since. Maybe they are still waiting for me to call once again on their queer and terrible names. (7)

Buechner implies that Jacob's connection to the idols is more than physical. Though they are buried, they may still have a hold on him, like the addiction of toxic shame. It is only as he develops his relationship with God that the influence of the gods will not be seductive. Idols are anything which take the place of God. "Idolatry," writes Buechner in *Wishful Thinking: A Theological A B C*,

> is the practice of ascribing absolute value to things of relative worth. Under certain circumstances money, patriotism, sexual freedom, moral principles, family loyalty, physical health, social or intellectual preeminence, and so on are fine things to have around, but to make them the

standard by which all other values are measured, to make them your masters, to look to them to justify your life and save your soul is sheerest folly. They just aren't up to it. (40)

Similarly, in *Shattering the Gods Within*, Allen notes that

> in the New Testament idols were associated with various human appetites such as covetousness, lust, and greed (Ephesians 5:5, Philippians 3:19). In essence an idol is anything that is given ultimate value and worshipped in place of God the Holy One. . . . In modern culture, however, the situation is more confusing and the concept of idolatry or pseudo gods is less well defined. . . . Confronting a deep sense of inadequacy because of the overwhelming challenges facing us, we become self-absorbed and create powerful, unconscious images of ourselves. Seeking tangible forms of meaning for our lives, we become vulnerable to create idols and pseudo gods by projecting our narcissistic images onto surrounding reality. . . . Idols and pseudo gods are made in our heart. (10-11, 12)

Seen in this broader perspective, it is clear that the burial of the gods is of central importance in the development of Israel's commitment to God. Buechner has *The Son of Laughter* begin with this event, then segue into the role the gods played in Laban's life. Only in the eighth chapter do we come to appreciate how central his burial of the gods is as an indication of Israel's spiritual growth. It occurs after he has wrestled with the unnamed one by the river Jabbok and received the name Israel, which dramatizes his change in relinquishing the safety net of the old ways, Laban's gods, and his own manipulations. Yet for Buechner's Israel, this breaking with the past has a price, for linked in his mind with the burial of the gods are the deaths of Rachel's nurse and his wife Rachel during childbirth.

Similar to the inverted chronology in *Godric,* which shows the protagonist as an old man listening to his life, Buechner changes the order in which the events are recounted to illustrate Jacob's spiritual and psychological development. The past is not neatly compartmentalized, but tends to merge with the present. Memories of shame bring a realization of God's continued blessing. As Allen has described in the therapeutic process, one must walk the hurt trail in order to discover the love story. Israel is looking back, reexperiencing his shame, but also seeing the hand of God holding and guiding in spite of his failings.

A change takes place as Heels becomes Israel, "one who strives with God and man and perseveres." Buechner might add "one who strives with himself and comes to accept God's grace." For Buechner, the issue is not sin, shame or hurt, but what one does with these. Shame is the human condition. The natural reaction is to cover up, to hide, to avoid exposure. As Buechner explains in *Telling Secrets*, healing comes as one faces the hurt, the shame, the secret, and in admitting it, one receives forgiveness and healing. This is the purpose of therapy, the purpose of confession. Thus *The Son of Laughter* is Jacob's confession, his retrospective examination of his hurt trail, the process by which he discovers the mystery of God's love. As Joseph thinks to himself near the end of the novel:

> And sometimes in the night he thought that the remembering was better than the forgetting because to forget the griefs was to forget also the gifts born out of the griefs like the life of his brother Benjamin born out of his mother's death, and his own rise to great power born out of the pit where his brothers had cast him. The Fear had two hands, he thought, one of them a hand that takes away

and the other a hand that gives as a father gives to
a child he has brought to sorrow. (253)

As psychological indicators, dreams have been important in Buechner's novels. In the Jacob narratives dreams are more than psychological messages from the unconscious; they are direct messages from God. Jacob's dream of the angels ascending and descending the stone stair reconfirms God's promise. Joseph's dreams of the sun and moon bowing and the sheaves of wheat bowing are symbolically prophetic and are fulfilled. Joseph's accurate interpretation of dreams leads to his rise in Egypt. As in the biblical narratives, dreams are a direct access to the spiritual: they predict and confirm promises of God for the present and the future.

In his other novels, dreams are often a highway to the unconscious. Antonio Parr's dreams on the train reveal his unconscious preoccupations, and his concerns regarding exposure, and the Lone Ranger dreams reveal his openness to the spiritual dimension. Dreams may reveal truths which are messages to ourselves, such as Buechner's own dream about a room called remember (TS 65). In his dreams Godric experiences visions which tell him truths about himself and what he should do. In *The Son of Laughter*, Buechner includes the biblical dreams, accepted at face value as a direct revelation from God to Jacob and Joseph. By presenting the supernatural as literal fact in Jacob's experience, as the visions are in Godric's, Buechner injects a willing suspension of rational and psychological explanation.

Buechner includes the dream material from the scriptures in *The Son of Laughter* as direct spiritual messages. In *The Book of Bebb* dreams were a mixture of psychological and spiritual revelations seeping into the conscious mind. Assimilating Freud's theory of the unconscious, in which only a small part of our internal reality is known to the conscious mind, Buechner seeks to reveal the ways this inner spiritual reality also breaks forth—through intuitions, impressions, hunches, tears, and dreams. Thus in

Buechner's psychological spirituality, dreams may be a ladder to God, a highway to our unconscious, or both.

Part II "The Dreaming" is Israel's "dream" account of what happened to his son Joseph. The dream of the pit and the dream of the Black Land provide a rather straightforward account of the material in the Jacob narratives (with some embellishments which are not directly related to Jacob). As Israel is reunited with Joseph in Egypt, the themes of promising and dreaming are brought together. For Buechner, the mystery of the life of faith is this interconnection: God may reveal his promise through dreams, though the promise is often beyond our power to grasp; like a dream it is elusive. Yet like the unconscious, as revealed in dreams, it may hold the secrets of our past and present. Poetically, Buechner has the novel end with Israel's musing on the mysterious interaction of promise and dream:

> As Joseph said, "He [the Fear] speaks to us sometimes in dreams that are like torches to light our way through the dark. He gives us daughters and sons so our seed may live after us and the promises he has made us may be kept to the world's luck and blessing." Perhaps that is enough.
>
> The night in Beersheba when he said that he would be with me in the Black Land, he promised that he would bring me out again. Who knows the full meaning of his words? Who knows from how far he will bring me and to what place even farther still?
>
> Is his promise only a dream?
>
> Is it in our dreaming that we glimpse the fullness of his promise? (273-274)

These last two questions capture Buechner's approach to psychological spirituality. The first, "Is his promise only a dream?"

expresses the continuing paradox of faith coexisting with doubt; the second, drawing on the role of the unconscious and the mystery in psychological and spiritual life, offers the possibility of an affirmation: In our dreaming (the unconscious subliminal level of intuition) we may glimpse the fullness of his promise.

In Buechner's open-ended way, the revelation of God's presence may be discovered in searching out the unconscious or the place where dreams come from, through psychotherapy, dream analysis, meditation, communing with nature, reading scripture, hearing a sermon, writing a novel, participating in a recovery group, or in listening attentively to one's past and present experiences. In Buechner's psychological spirituality, it is by listening to one's life, with the ears of the heart, that one discerns God's alphabet of grace.

Appendix to Chapter 6

Jacob's Identity in the Christian and Literary Worlds

Buechner's emphasis on the "fair and foul" mixture in Jacob is compatible with twentieth-century psychological understanding of humanity and lack of hero idealization, but is a departure from the traditional biblical view of Jacob and the typological interpretation of the early church fathers. In the New Testament, Jacob is referred to four times: by the Samaritan woman who assumes Jesus is not "greater than our father Jacob who gave us the well and drank of it himself, and his sons and his cattle" (John 4:12); by St. Stephen before his martyrdom as he recounts the history of the children of Israel and of Jacob's being the father of the twelve patriarchs (Acts 7:8-16); by St. Paul as exemplifying the sovereignty of God, chosen as the child of promise (Romans 9:10-13)[2], and by the author of the letter to the Hebrews as an example of an Old Testament hero who lived by faith (Hebrews 11:9, 20-22).

Early Christian church fathers went a step further and in gleaning typological lessons from the Old Testament, viewed Jacob as a type of "redeemed Israel" and of Christ. Commenting on the verse "Jacob have I loved, but Esau have I hated" (Mal. 1:2;

Rom. 9:13), St. Irenaeus sees him as typifying the Christian church (replacing the Jews as God's chosen) and also as a type of Christ with his twelve apostles:

> If any one . . . will look into Jacob's actions, he shall find them . . . full of import with regard to the dispensations. Thus, in the first place, at his birth, since he laid hold of his brother's heel, he was called "Jacob," that is, the "supplanter"— one who holds but is not held . . . striving and conquering . . . . For to this end was the Lord born, the type of whose birth he set forth beforehand . . . . In the next place he received the rights of the firstborn, when his brother looked on them with contempt; even as also the younger nation received Him, Christ, the first-begotten, when the elder nation rejected Him, saying, "We have no king but Caesar." In Christ every blessing is summed up, and therefore the latter people has snatched away the blessings of the former from the Father, just as Jacob took away the blessing of his brother Esau . . . . In a foreign country were the twelve tribes born, the race of Israel, inasmuch as Christ also was to generate, in a strange country, the twelve-pillared foundation [the twelve disciples] of the Church. Various colored sheep were allotted to Jacob as his wages; and the wages of Christ are human beings, who from various and diverse nations come together in one fold of faith. (in Adversus haereses (21.3) from Jeffrey, A *Dictionary of Biblical Tradition in English Literature* 386)

St. Augustine, in keeping with early Christian tradition, saw Jacob as a type of the Church and justified his underhanded behavior: "That which he did at his mother's bidding, so as to seem to deceive his father, if with diligence and faith it be attended to, is no lie, but a mystery" (Contra mendacium, 24 quoted in Jeffrey, *A Dictionary of Biblical Tradition in English Literature* 386). Ambrose goes further in seeing Jacob as a type of Christ to be followed in his obedience to his mother and service to his father-in-law: "In Jacob, too, let us imitate the type of Christ" (De excessu, 22 in Jeffrey 386) Throughout the Middle Ages when the Old Testament was interpreted allegorically, Jacob's typological connection with Christ had become a commonplace.

The traditional hagiographic approach to Jacob emphasized his exemplary behavior. Chaucer cites Jacob as an example of wisdom and the blessings of obedience: "Loo, Jacob, by good counseil of his mooder Rebekka, wan the benysoun of Ysaak his fader, and the lordshipe over alle his brethren" (The Tale of Melibee, 7.2285-87). In *The Canterbury Tales*, a masterly depiction of humanity both "fair and foul," Chaucer implies Rebekah's was deceitful counsel in "The Merchant's Tale." Exhibiting her clever ability to twist scripture for her own purposes, the Wife of Bath cites the story of Jacob as her rationale for her multiple marriages in the Prologue (Jeffrey 386).

This interpretative strategy also took on an anti-semitic slant. St. Augustine saw "The elder shall serve the younger" as signifying that the Jews will serve their younger sibling, the Christians (De civ. Dei 16.35), an interpretation shared by Cornelius a Lapide, the Counter-Reformation commentator. In literature Jacob's Jewish characteristics were stereotyped. In Shakespeare's Merchant of Venice, Shylock views Jacob as a role model in enterprise, swearing "by Jacob's staff" (2.5.36 cf.1.3.68-97).

With the Protestant emphasis on justification by faith, Jacob is seen more as an example of sovereign grace than meritorious service and his human weakness is emphasized (a view similar to Buechner's). Cranmer and Coverdale focus more on Jacob's moral limitations (symbolized in his leaning on his staff in Genesis 32:10). In his "Sermon Preached at Whitehall, April 12, 1618"

John Donne cites Jacob's prayer at the fording of the Jabbok as a confession and "the establishment of all true prayers, a disclaiming of Merit." Jacob's coming to rely on God's electing grace rather than his own strength is thus central to his spiritual identity.

This shift from sanctifying Jacob to seeing his moral frailty as his identifying link to humanity is captured by John Donne in "Holy Sonnet 11" with an ironic twist:

> And Jacob came cloth'd in vile harsh attire
> But to supplant, and with gainfull intent;
> God cloth'd himself in vile man's flesh, that so
> Hee might be weake enough to suffer woe.

Seeing types in the story of Jacob is adapted by Vaughan to a contemporary situation in "Jacob's Pillow, and Pillar" The dispute between Jacob and Esau parallels the English Civil War, with the stone pillow as a type fulfilled in Christ who comforts even in the time of strife between brothers.

Like Buechner's perspective of God's grace made perfect in weakness, Jacob's identification with humanity's weakness brings hope in Herrick's poem "Beggars" (1648),

> Jacob God's Beggar was; and so we wait
> (Though ne're so rich) all beggars at his gate.

The negative aspect of Jacob's character finds echoes in other twentieth century writers, most notably Ernest Hemingway. Just prior to the publication of *The Sun Also Rises* (1926), Hemingway changed the name of the protagonist from Ernest to Jacob. Wounded in the groin, this combative, struggling character is a "devout cynic" whose identity with Jacob is underscored when he is told, "You've a hell of a biblical name, Jake." Hemingway was at odds with his evangelical upbringing, and this substitution for his own name is significant personally as well as literarily.

More in keeping with Buechner's perspective of spiritual

paradox, in "The Jereboa" Marianne Moore highlights the mixture of fair and foul, heaven and earth in Jacob by comparing him to the pestiferous yet wiley "sand-brown jumping rat-free born":

> Part terrestrial
> and part celestial,
> Jacob saw, cudgel staff
> in claw hand—steps of air and angels; his
> friends were the desert stones. The translucent mistake
> of the desert, does not make
> hardship for one who
> can rest and then do
> the opposite.

The modernist anti-hero, characterized by ambivalence and paradox, often reflects the contemporary psychological understanding of alienation and shame, but without redemptive spirituality. Buechner's Heels thus develops quite naturally from the raw material in the Jacob narratives to reflect the author's unique psychological and spiritual perspective.

Notes

1 For a discussion of toxic shame see John Bradshaw, *Healing the Shame That Binds You*. Deerfield Beach, Florida: Health Communications, Inc., 1988.

2 Romans 9:10-13 reads . . . Rebekah also, when she had conceived twins by one man, our father Isaac; for though the twins were not yet born, and had not done anything good or bad, in order that God's purpose according to His choice might stand, not because of works, but because of Him who calls, it was said to her, "The older will serve the younger." Just as it is written, "Jacob I loved, but Esau I hated" (reference to Malachi 1:2-4).

3 But blessed *Jacob*, though thy sad distress
Was just the same with ours, and nothing less,
For thou a brother, and blood-thirsty too
Didst flye, whose children wrought thy childrens wo:
Yet thou in all thy solitude and grief,
On stones didst sleep and found'st but cold relief:
Thou from the Day-star a long way didst stand
And all that distance was Law and command.
But we a healing Sun by day and night,
Have our sure Guardian, and our leading light;
What thou didst hope for and believe, we finde
And feel a friend most ready, sure and kinde.
Thy pillow was but type and shade at best,
But we the substance have, and on him rest.

7

Buechner's Psychological Spirituality in a Postmodern World

Describing the changes from modernism to postmodernism in 1992, Vaclav Havel,[1] then-President of Czechoslovakia, stated that the end of Communism was a message signifying the "end not just to the nineteenth and twentieth centuries, but to the modern age." Havel explained:

> The modern era has been dominated by the culminating belief, expressed in different forms, that the world—and Being as such—is a wholly knowable system governed by a finite number of universal laws that man can grasp and rationally direct for his own benefit. This era, beginning in the Renaissance and developing from the Enlightenment to socialism, from positivism to scientism, from the Industrial Revolution to the information revolution, was characterized by rapid advances in rational, cognitive thinking . . . . It was an era in which there was a cult of

depersonalized objectivity, an era in which objective knowledge was amassed and technologically exploited, an era of belief in automatic progress brokered by the scientific method....

What is needed is something different, something larger. Man's attitude to the world must be radically changed.... We must try harder to understand than to explain. The way forward is not in the mere construction of universal systemic solutions, to be applied to reality from the outside; it is also *in seeking to get to the heart of reality through personal experience.... In a word, human uniqueness, human action and the human spirit must be rehabilitated....*

[A politician] *must trust not only an objective interpretation of reality, but also his own soul*; not only an adopted ideology, but also his own thoughts; not only the summary reports he receives each morning, but also his own feeling.

Soul, individual spirituality, first hand personal insight into things; the courage to be himself and go the way his conscience points, humility in the face of the mysterious order of Being, confidence in its natural direction and, above all, trust in his own subjectivity as his principal link with the subjectivity of the world—these are the qualities that politicians of the future should cultivate. [Italics mine]

In words echoing the dynamics of Buechner's psychological approach to spirituality, Vaclav Havel foresees a move away from faith in "objective theoretical truth" to a greater trust in individual experience, a transition from the modern to the postmodern perspective.[2] What he is describing parallels the development from

BUECHNER'S PSYCHOLOGICAL SPIRITUALITY IN A POSTMODERN WORLD

Buechner's earlier modernist works to his later novels which incorporates personal spirituality and psychological acuity.

His earliest novel *A Long Day's Dying* focuses on the alienation facing sophisticated moderns, especially Tristram Bone, who is unable to find meaning and relationships in an empty universe of façades and mistrust. The Waste Land of modernism is the essence of this novel of the 1950s. Later Buechner sought to convey the value of mystical or visionary experience in *The Seasons' Difference*, but his novel was so far fetched critics felt it offered little in the way of convincing portrayal of characters or life. Seeking to create a place where the difficulties of modernism could be worked out, *The Return of Ansel Gibbs* wrestles with the "liberal narrative." Despite his awareness of the complexities of modern life, the protagonist decides to act to the best of his ability, having been encouraged by a caring community and a sense that something larger than himself may be involved.

The Final Beast sets the stage with the same sense of modern anxiety and ambivalence seen in the previous novels, but this time the faith commitment of the young minister, bolstered by the intervention of a wise and spiritual mentor, provides an alternative recourse for meaningful human and divine intervention in the lives of alienated characters. *Entrance to Porlock* uses the mythical Oz story to reach overarching truths about human existence, but like *The Seasons' Difference*, this book did not connect with the reality of most readers or critics.

In the *Book of Bebb* the two main characters objectify Buechner's emerging psychological-spiritual emphasis on listening to one's life. With ambivalence and doubt, the modernistic narrator meets the spiritual, yet fallible Leo Bebb. No longer is the despair of modernism the bottom line, although it is present throughout the novel. Bebb's zany, postmodern subjectivity within the context of the larger, traditional framework of Christianity, personifies the "soul, individual spirituality, first hand personal insight into things, the courage to be himself and go the way his conscience points" which Havel envisions. This "humility in the face of the mysterious order of Being" characterizes the spiritual experiences that defy purely logical explanation that Buechner incorporates in the lives of his protagonists. Individual spirituality revealed convincingly through a first-person narrator undergoing psychological and spiritual struggles reflects the essence of *Godric* and *Son of Laughter*. In both novels, "anti-heroic" vulnerable characters demonstrate the paradox of living by faith.

To portray the vibrant spiritual essence of the life of faith, the author draws on his own spiritual and psychological struggles, where he learned through painful and joyous experience, not theoretical abstraction. Thus the novels articulate many unconscious insights from the author's life. In keeping with Havel's analysis, the emphasis in listening to one's life is on "soul, individual spirituality, first hand personal insight into things." This speaks to a contemporary audience. It is not merely the personal outpourings of a romantic poet's angst; it is the articulate voice of one who has been through extensive psychotherapy and spiritual training, both in seminary and with spiritual directors, so his particular personal experience finds resonance in a wider context. In these novels, that which is most personal is universal, revealing developments from modernism to postmodernism as expressed through the imagination and inner consciousness, the *imago dei,* of Frederick Buechner.

Within the perspective of Buechner's entire corpus[3], his autobiographical journal *Alphabet of Grace,* his novel *Lion Country*, and his experience in psychotherapy deeply affect his subsequent approach to writing and to listening to his life.

When Buechner began to write this autobiographical journal seeing the events in daily life "as the alphabet through which God, of his grace, spells out his words, his meaning, to us" (NT 86), he expressed in writing what he had been trying to do in his own experience. Since his conversion he had been seeking to know God by listening to his own life as he experienced it day by day. Through psychotherapy, which would become more important later, he was seeking to listen to himself and to search his memory for the ways God was present in his past. For the first time he sought to record these attempts to listen to his life, and the result was *The Alphabet of Grace* (1970). In a new way, the structure of his writing paralleled his content, as he used a subjective and seemingly spontaneous autobiographical journal to note the intersecting spiritual and natural impressions of his daily experience.

In his stream of consciousness journal, we partake in the author's personal experience through flashbacks of memory, his feelings about his past, present, and future, his thoughts about God, his family and himself. Although he does not use the specific terminology, we are witnessing the author listening to his life, a theme in all Buechner's writings, but especially affecting the way he approaches his subject matter in his later novels. *Alphabet of Grace* marks a definitive shift in Buechner's writing in theme and style which was to leave a lasting imprint on all his subsequent work. Out of the same stylistic technique, a narrator listening to the random alphabet of his life, *Lion Country* and the subsequent Bebb novels were born.

Buechner says he learned about exposure and taking risks from Leo Bebb and was then able to expose himself in his own memoirs.[4] In an interview with W. Dale Brown in 1989, Buechner also reveals, "A lot of what went into *The Sacred Journey* I went through first with a therapist. And then I shed tears about it, but they were as tears usually are, wonderfully healing" (51).

The psychological value of self-exposure—remembering one's painful hurt trail to discover one's love story—which Buechner gained through psychotherapy, gives his later novels their superior force. *Godric* is a literary masterpiece. It is also a psychological revelation of the self-examined life, and writing it for Buechner was in itself a kind of therapy.

Buechner's growing transparency comes through his novels. Learning and growing from his own therapy in the 1970s, Buechner's insights about himself and life in general become more psychologically attuned. It is not that Buechner now consciously applies a more articulate psychological paradigm in his writing.

Rather it is because the author himself has changed that the writing is more alive and has more depth. Having experienced in therapy what it means to be a wounded healer, Buechner embodies in his characters the psychological and spiritual insights of psychotherapy and narrative theology. Insights alone do not make great literature, but in the hands of a superb writer, they provide the rich soil in which a literary craftsman can create. It is not the themes, or the psychology, or the spirituality, per se, but the ways Buechner expresses these through vivid characters which resonate with contemporary readers. It is the struggle of the self seen in Faulkner, Hemingway, and other novelists with many different styles, which captures something lasting and effective. As Buechner has said, all fiction, like all dreams, and like all theology, is at its heart symbolic autobiography (NT 81).

Notes

1 Address before the 1992 World Economic Forum in Davos, Switzerland, quoted in "The End of the Modern Era" *The New York Times* Op-Ed March 1, 1992.

2 According to Ken Wilber in *The Marriage of Sense and Soul: Integrating Science and Religion,* a narrow and technical definition of "postmodern" involves "the notion that there is no truth, only interpretation, and all interpretations are socially constructed." This view can be thought of as "extreme postmodernism" "because it takes certain very important insights (e.g., many realities are socially constructed) and blows them totally out of proportion (e.g., all realities are socially constructed), which results in nothing but severe performative contradictions."

"But in the broader and more general sense, 'postmodern' simply means any of the major currents occurring *in the wake of modernity*—as a reaction against modernity, or as counterbalance to modernity, or sometimes as a continuation of modernity by other means. Thus, if industrialization is modern, the information age is postmodern.... If perspectival rationality is modern, aperspectival network-logic is postmodern" (42-43). It is this broader definition which applies to aspects of Frederick Buechner's work.

3 As W. Dale Brown notes "Any attempt to compartmentalize neatly an artist's career into phases or stages or steps generally reduces or destroys the true power of that artist's work" (Diss 96). For example, scholars such as Brown, Engbers and Bruinooge have disputed Marie-Helene Davies' oversimplification that *The Final Beast*... is "the first" of his "religious novels." (3). Yet both W. Dale Brown and Nancy Myers contend that *Final Beast* is "the central work in the Buechner cannon" (Brown diss 160, Myers 75), though it continues themes of ambivalence, doubt, and

"symptoms of modernism" (Thompson diss 44).

4 Although he had referred to his father's suicide in fictional form in almost all his previous novels, and he specifically mentioned it in *Alphabet of Grace* in a flashback, he had never before written a detailed and self-revealing memoir of his life.

Fiction by Frederick Buechner (chronological order)

Abbreviations

A Long Day's Dying. New York: Alfred A. Knopf, 1950.	LDD
The Seasons' Difference. New York: Alfred A. Knopf, 1952.	SD
The Return of Ansel Gibbs. New York: Alfred A. Knopf, 1958.	RAG
The Final Beast. New York: Atheneum, 1965; San Francisco: Harper & Row, 1982.	FB
The Entrance to Porlock. New York: Atheneum, 1970.	ETP
Lion Country. New York: Atheneum, 1971; San Francisco: Harper & Row, 1984.	LC
Open Heart. New York: Atheneum, 1972; San Francisco: Harper & Row, 1984.	OH
Love Feast. New York: Atheneum, 1974; San Francisco: Harper & Row, 1984.	LF
Treasure Hunt. New York: Atheneum, 1977; San Francisco: Harper & Row, 1984.	TH
The Book of Bebb. New York: Atheneum, 1979; San Francisco: HarperCollins, 1990.	BB
Godric. New York: Atheneum, 1980; San Francisco: Harper & Row, 1983.	
Brendan. New York: Atheneum, 1987; San Francisco: Harper & Row, 1988.	
The Wizard's Tide. San Francisco: HarperCollins, 1990.	WT
The Son of Laughter. San Francisco: HarperCollins, 1993.	SON
On the Road with the Archangel. San Francisco: HarperCollins, 1997.	
The Storm. San Francisco: HarperCollins, 1998.	

LISTENING TO LIFE

Non-Fiction by Frederick Buechner (chronological order)

Abbreviations

The Magnificent Defeat. New York: Seabury Press, 1966. San Francisco: Harper & Row, 1985.	MD
The Hungering Dark. New York: Seabury Press, 1969. San Francisco: Harper & Row, 1985.	HD
The Alphabet of Grace. New York: Seabury Press, 1970; San Francisco: Harper & Row, 1985.	AG
Wishful Thinking: A Theological ABC. New York: Harper and Row, 1973.	WT
The Faces of Jesus. New York: Simon and Schuster, 1974; San Francisco: Harper & Row, 1989.	
Telling the Truth: The Gospel as Tragedy, Comedy and Fairy Tale. San Francisco: Harper and Row, 1977.	TT
Peculiar Treasures: A Biblical Who's Who. San Francisco: Harper and Row, 1979.	PT
The Sacred Journey. San Francisco: Harper and Row, 1982.	SJ
Now and Then. San Francisco: Harper and Row, 1983.	NT
A Room Called Remember. San Francisco: Harper and Row, 1984.	RCR
Whistling in the Dark: *An ABC Theologized.* San Francisco: Harper and Row, 1988	WD
Telling Secrets: A Memoir. San Francisco: HarperCollins, 1991.	TS
The Clown in the Belfry: Writings on Faith and Fiction. San Francisco: HarperCollins, 1992.	
Listening to Your Life: Daily Meditations with Frederick Buechner. Compiled by George Connor. San Francisco: HarperCollins, 1992.	
The Longing for Home. San Francisco: HarperCollins, 1996.	
The Eyes of the Heart: A Memoir of the Lost and Found. San Francisco: HarperCollins, 1999.	
Speak What We Feel (Not What We Ought to Say): Reflections on Literature and Faith. San Francisco: HarperCollins, 2001.	

Listening to Life

Works Cited

Abrams, M. H. *A Glossary of Literary Terms.* 6th ed. NY: Harcourt Brace, 1993.

Adams, P. L. rev. of *Godric. Atlantic Monthly* 246 Dec. 1980 96.

Aldridge, John W. *After the Lost Generation: A Critical Study of the Writers of Two Wars.* McGraw, 1951.

Allen, David F. *In Search of the Heart: The Road to Spiritual Discovery.* Forward by Henri Nouwen. Nashville: Thomas Nelson, 1993.

—. *Shattering the Gods Within.* Chicago: Moody, 1994.

Allen, David F., and Robert Bachelder. "Psychiatry and Religion: Judeo-Christian Theism and Fromm's Humanism." *Journal of Religion and Health.* Vol. 24. No. 1. Spring, 1985. 49-59.

Anderson, Chris. "The Very Style of Faith: Frederick Buechner as Homilist and Essayist." *Christianity and Literature* 38:2 (Winter 1989): 7-21.

Auchincloss, Douglas. *"The Son of Laughter"* rev. *Parabola* 18 (1993) 95-96.

"Buechner, (Carl) Frederick 1926- ." *Contemporary Authors: New Revision Series.* 11 (1984): 104-110 (interview); 39 (1993): 46-51.

Baxter, Harold Jason. "Touched by Fire and Laughter: The Range of Grace in the Fiction of Flannery O'Connor and Frederick Buechner." Diss. Florida State U, 1983.

Bible: Revised Standard Version, 1946, 1952, 1971, 1973. King James Version, and New American Standard Version, 1960, 1977.

Brown, W. Dale. "Frederick Buechner: An Introduction." Diss. U of Missouri-Columbia, 1987.

—. *Of Fiction and Faith: Twelve American Writers Talk about Their Vision And Work.* Grand Rapids, MI: Wm. B. Eerdmans, 1997.

—. "To Be A Saint: Frederick Buechner's *The Final Beast* and Rewriting Graham Greene." *Religion and Literature* 24.2 (Summer 1992): 51-65.

Bruinooge, Nathan, and Chad Engbers. "Frederick Buechner's *Godric*: Sinner and Saint Recomplicated." *CEA MAGazine* 199: 35-49.

Christianity Today "1994 Book Awards: Critics'-Choice Book Awards," April 4, 1994, 41.

Crews, Frederick. *The Critics Bear It Away: American Fiction and the Academy.* NY: Random House, 1992.

Daiches, David. "Widow on a College Campus." *New York Times Book Review* Jan. 8, 1950: 4.

Davenport, Guy. *New York Times Book Review* Feb. 14, 1971: 7.

Davenport, John. "Buechner's Fourth." *Spectator.* June 11, 1965: 763.

Davies, Horton. "Frederick Buechner and the Strange Work of Grace."

Theology Today 36 Jul 1979: 186-194.

Davies, Horton and Marie-Helen Davies. "The God of Storm and Stillness: The Fiction of Flannery O'Connor and Frederick Buechner." *Religion in Life* (Summer 1979): 188-196.

Davies, Marie Helene. *Laughter in a Genevan Gown: The Works of Frederick Buechner 1970-1980*. Grand Rapids, MI: Wm. B. Eerdmans, 1983.

Dinges, William D. "Postmodernism and Religious Institutions." *The Way*. July 1996: 215-224.

Dillard, Annie, "The Ancient Story of Jacob, retold in a passionate, exalted pitch." *Boston Sunday Globe* May 30, 1993: A15.

"Dove on Wires." *Newsweek* Jan.25, 1965: 92-4.

Doyle, Paul A. rev. of *Lion Country*. *Best Sellers* March 1, 1971: 54.

Gibble, Kenneth L. "Listening to My Life: An Interview with Frederick Buechner." *Christian Century* 100 Nov. 16, 1983: 1042-1045.

Green, Howar. *Hudson Review*. 18 (Summer 65) 285-286.

Hassan, Ihab. *Radical Innocence: Studies in the Contemporary Novel*. Princeton UP, 1961.

Havel, Vaclav. "The End of the Modern Era" speech reprinted in *New York Times* OP-ED March 1, 1992.

Inderbitzin, Lawrence B. and Mark E. James. "Psychoanalytic Psychology." *Human Behavior: An Introduction for Medical Students*. Ed. Alan Stoudemire. 2nd ed. New York: Lippincott-Raven, 1997.

Jeffrey, David Lyle. *A Dictionary of Biblical Tradition in English Literature*. Grand Rapids, MI: Wm. B. Eerdmans, 1992.

Jones, James W. *Contemporary Psychoanalysis and Religion: Transference and Transcendence*. New Haven: Yale UP, 1991.

Keating, Thomas. *Intimacy with God*. NY Crossroad, 1994.

—. *Open Mind, Open Heart: The Contemplative Dimension of the Gospel*. Rockport, MA Element, 1986.

Kelsey, Morton. *Dreams: A Way to Listen to God*. NY Paullist P, 1978.

Lewis, Michael. *Shame: The Exposed Self*. NY: The Free Press Simon &Schuster,Inc. 1992.

Lewis, Peter. "Lives of the Saint." *Times Literary Supplement* (Mar. 13, 1981) 278.

McCoy, Marjorie C., *Frederick Buechner: Novelist and Theologian of the Lost and Found*. San Francisco: Harper and Row, 1988.

Malin, Irving, "Words Fail Me: *The Son of Laughter*," *Commonweal* July, 16, 1993:27.

Malony, H. Newton, and Bernard Spilka, eds. *Religion in Psychodynamic Perspective:*

The Contributions of Paul W. Pruyser. Oxford: Oxford UP, 1991.

May, Gerald G. *Care of Mind/Care of Spirit: A Psychiatrist Explores Spiritual Direction.* San Francisco: Harper and Row, 1982.

—. *Will and Spirit: A Contemplative Psychology.* San Francisco: Harper and Row, 1982.

May, John R. Rev. of *Godric. America* 144:16 (Apr. 25, 1981): 348.

Meng, Heinrich, and Ernest Freud. *Psychoanalysis and Faith: The Letters of Sigmund Freud and Oskar Pfister,* ed. New York: Basic Books, 1963.

Mellin, John O. rev. of *The Final Beast. Theology Today* 40. (Apr. 83): 103.

Merton, Thomas. *Seeds of Contemplation.* NY: New Directions Pub. Co., 1949, 1986.

—. *The Waters of Siloe.* NY: Harcourt and Brace, 1949.

Moynahan, Julian "Writing on cloth can be tricky" rev. of *The Final Beast. Book Week* Feb. 14, 1965: 6-8.

Myers, Nancy Beth. "Sanctifying the Profane: Religious Themes in the Fiction of Frederick Buechner." Diss. North Texas State U, 1976.

Nelson, Shirley and Rudy. Rev. of *Godric.* "Buechner: Novelist to 'Cultural [sic] Despisers.'" *Christianity Today* 25 May 29, 1981: 44.

Neuman, Matthias, O.S.B. "The Religious Structure of a Spirituality." *American Benedictine Review* 33 June, 1982: 115-148.

Nicholi, Armand. "Hope in a Secular Age." *Finding God at Harvard: Spiritual Journeys of Thinking Christians.* Kelly Monroe, ed. Grand Rapids, MI: Zondervan, 1996.

Nouwen, Henri J. M. *The Wounded Healer.* New York: Doubleday, 1972.

Ozick, Cynthia. "Open Heart." *New York Times Book Review* Jun 11, 1972: 4+.

Peterson, Eugene H. "The Son of Laughter." *Theology Today.* 50. 607-610.

Podhoretz, Norman. "The New Nihilism and the Novel," *Partisan Review.* XXV. Fall, 1958: 576-90.

Prescott, Peter. "Holy Man With a Past." *Newsweek* Nov. 10, 1980: 112-114.

Price, Emerson. "*A Long Day's Dying* Shows Rare Wisdom." *Cleveland Press* Jan. 10, 1950: 24.

Schaub, Thomas Hill. *American Fiction in the Cold War.* Madison, WI: Wisconsin UP, 1991.

Sendry, Joseph. "1993 CCL Book Award Citation." *Christianity and Literature.* 42:2 Winter 1993 378-9.

Spectorsky, A. C. rev. of *The Return of Ansel Gibbs. Saturday Review of Literature.* Feb. 15, 1958. 21.

Stoudemire, Alan, ed. *Human Behavior: An Introduction for Medical Students* 2nd ed.

Philadelphia PA: Lippincott-Raven., 1997.

Tanner, Tony. *The Reign of Wonder: Naivety and Reality in American Literature.* Cambridge: Cambridge UP, 1965.

Tennyson, G.B., and Edward E. Ericson, Jr.,eds. *Religion and Modern Literature: Essays in Theory and Criticism.* Grand Rapids, Michigan: William B. Eerdman's, 1975.

Thompson, Stacy Webb. "The Rediscovery of Wonder: A Critical Introduction to the Novels of Frederick Buechner." Diss. Michigan State U, 1979.

Tilley, Terence W. with John Edwards et. al. *Postmodern Theologies: The Challenge of Religious Diversity.* Maryknoll, NY: Orbis Books, 1995.

Wilber, Ken. *The Marriage of Sense and Soul: Integrating Science and Religion.* NY: Random House 1998.

Wilder, Amos. "Strategies of the Christian Artist." *Christianity and Crisis* 25 1965: 92-95.

Woelfel, James. "Frederick Buechner: The Novelist as Theologian." *Theology Today* 40 Oct 1983: 273-291.